Love, an

Inner Connection

Love, an Inner Connection

Based on Principles Drawn from the I Ching

Second Edition

by Carol K. Anthony

ISBN 1-890764-01-9
Library of Congress Catalog Card Number 2002090717
Anthony Publishing Company
206 Gleasondale Road
Stow, Massachusetts 01775
www.ichingoracle.com
1st edition published in 1993. Second edition 2002.
Printed in the United States of America
Cover & Text Design by Leslie Carlson
Cover photo by Luz Anthony

Table of Contents

Preface to the Second Edition

❧

Circumstances quite beyond my control decided that I should produce a new edition of this book, first published in 1993. The printer moved and lost the flats, and my designer no longer could open her old computer file with the cover on it. I did, however, have the text, and it was even in a ready-for-print computer format. Because I was in the middle of another project, I thought I could simply prepare it again for print, as it was.

However, as I began entering some minor corrections that were needed, I revisited the text and saw that a few changes could be made to improve it. One change led to another, until "voila!" a new edition was underway.

If I have learned anything over the years, it is that the Sage is always enlarging my viewpoint. One realization is always followed by another, bigger one. It has been somewhat like climbing a mountain, one hand-hold after another. Each hand-hold has become the basis for another stretch upward, which has led to a yet broader view. There is no end to learning, no ultimate stopping place. This second edition is to share some of what I have learned since 1993 that impacts the love relationship.

One of the new realizations was the *I Ching* meaning of "taking action." Like all action counselled by the *I Ching*, it refers to inner, rather than outer action; in particular it refers to the saying of an inner No to something that is incorrect. This realization was such an important breakthrough for me, when it occurred, that I planned to write an entire book about the inner No. It was not meant to be, however. Instead, the inner No is now incorporated into an entirely new version of the *I Ching* that I have been working on with my colleague, Hanna Moog. Many of the other changes I have inserted here have come from our working on this new book.

Other changes have come from discovering more about the nature of the ego and its workings in the psyche. Inasmuch as it is bound up in the entire hierarchical structuring of human relationships, I have ceased to use hierarchical terms that are common in the *I Ching* and in our language, such as "higher" and "lower," "superior" and "inferior." Due to what we have learned from the Sage in writing the new *I Ching*, we have also removed the word "power" in connection with the Cosmos upon learning that our presumption that the Cosmos works through power was incorrect. It made us aware that the use of power is the way the ego works, and that the Cosmos works only through the attraction of complementary aspects. Another word for this attraction is love.

A still further enlargement of our view came with understanding that the Cosmos is a feeling consciousness, and *everything* in nature is compressed consciousness. This fact, hinted at in the first edition, did not become a full-blown realization until later. It is because the Cosmos is made up of consciousness that what we think and feel is of such great significance, for when we think and feel in ways that are against the Cosmic harmony, we separate from our unity with the Cosmos and lose its protection and help.

Other changes have to do with the development of a better and more thorough understanding of the ego. I have come to recognize that it is the product of the feudal mindset that has dominated our thinking for the last 3,000 years. This mindset is not merely *like* a computer program, it *is* a false internal program we have taken in that works in precisely the same way that computer programs do. We have since learned techniques to deprogram it, and in doing so, have found a much more effective way of ending problems in relationships.

I wish to thank all the readers who have taken the time to share their appreciation of the first edition. I wish here to thank my colleague, Hanna Moog, for her expert help in editing and preparing this new edition. I also thank my daughter Leslie Anthony Bowen, for the cover and book design, and my daughter-in-law Luz Anthony, for the photo of Lago Garda.

Carol K. Anthony
February, 2002

Preface to the First Edition

In my book, *The Philosophy of the I Ching*, (Anthony Publishing Company, 1981) I wrote a small chapter describing the *I Ching*'s central concepts regarding relationships called "Coming to Meet Halfway." Through being asked many questions on this subject over the intervening years, and finding it impossible to answer these questions adequately in the short space of lectures, I began to see the need to elaborate on these principles in a book.

The more I thought about it, the more I saw that contemporary relationships have departed ever further from these Cosmic principles, causing much suffering.

At first I planned to discuss relationships in general, merely elaborating on that earlier chapter. After writing twenty-two chapters, however, I began to realize that I had only circled the main issue. I began to see that only by beginning anew and addressing the way we relate on the most intimate level, could I find the model that is necessary to correct all relationships. The matter, I saw, lay not in the external ways we relate to others, but in the inner life of the heart from which externals emanate. This is because our deepest feelings and thoughts determine whether our relationships succeed or fail. This book, therefore, is about the inner life of the heart as it loves and responds to love, for it is here, in the heart, and not in the mind, that we live or fail to live. Relationships that do not involve the heart are bound to remain superficial and external.

The principles of relating described in this book are Cosmic and psychological in nature. As I mention in the introduction, the Chinese do not speak of love as we do. Neither do they admit to having had a psychology, but it will be seen that many views expressed in this book are derived from a superior psychology embedded in the *I Ching.* Although these principles are ancient, and phrased in ancient metaphors, they contain insights into the human psyche that we are only now, at this point in our history, discovering. These principles do not dispute current psychology but rather clarify and add to it. The reader will note, for example, that the *I Ching* concept of ego is in agreement with that held by some of the psychoanalytical writers of our age, such as Karen Horney and Harry Stack Sullivan.

By confining my discussion to the closest and most intimate relationship, I believe I will fulfill my larger aim of demonstrating the workings of the old Chinese maxim, which says, "If you want to correct the world, you must correct the community; if you want to correct the community, you must correct the family; if you want to correct the family, you must correct the husband-wife relationship; if you want to correct that, you must correct yourself." In my view, if we want a better, kinder, more loving world, we need, individually, to learn how to open our hearts to love, and thereby to being loved. If love is not in our lives, if we find ourselves trapped in relationships that are endlessly unkind, if we want the world to be better, more humane, more tender, we, and we alone, possess the means, within ourselves, to change these things. We cannot achieve this through logical or theoretical means, but through rectifying our most important, intimate relationships. By removing the barriers of fear that we have placed around our loving, we can help others around us remove their barriers. Once we begin to witness how this is possible in small and seemingly insignificant ways, we will begin to change the whole world.

We hardly need, in these times of high crime, divorce rate, teenage pregnancy, drug and alcohol addiction, poverty, war, and decadence, to point out the need to heal society. In view of the magnitude of the problem, it would seem that we would be required to alter ourselves drastically. This is not the case, however, for the wisdom of the *I Ching* makes it clear that it is enough to find, and become true to, our innermost true selves. Doing this accomplishes everything that is necessary to heal society.

The changes we need to make do not require us to become something special; they require only that we reunite with our true selves that we have repressed through conditioning. This ends the otherwise continuous inner conflict that results when we adopt or accept views that are untrue to our natures. What we achieve through work on ourselves is freedom from ideas that block our natural abilities to receive and give love in an open reciprocity. In addition, we reopen our natural connection to the loving Cosmos from which we have become isolated through fear, doubt, and hopelessness. Reconnecting with this marvelous energy, we discover how it overflows constantly to those around us in an unending, healing stream of energy. As we learn to do this, we take positive action toward halting the growing alienation and hopelessness that disturbs the world, that cripples us as individuals, and leaves us isolated from each other. Doing this we learn to love ourselves better, and in the process find ourselves able to give and receive love from others.

Having taken up this subject, I continued the practice I have always followed when writing about anything involving the *I Ching*, namely, I meditated every morning, then consulted the *I Ching*. Not only did it answer obvious questions, it began to define the questions, and to point out areas of further inquiry that I had not before considered. Moreover, this theoretical work was accompanied by real life experiences that happened synchronously, it seemed, to bring these points home. This did not surprise me, since this has always been the way that I have been taught by the Sage who speaks through the *I Ching*.

Many times I received Hexagram 42, Line 4, which speaks of "removing the capital." This refers to the habit kings had in ancient China of removing the capital of the country to a new location. Sometimes this happened when there was a change in dynasties, but sometimes it was done to free the government from entrenched patterns of acting and responding. One day, in meditation, I saw what it would be like if one suddenly moved the capital of the United States from Washington, D. C., to Peoria, Illinois. The special phone lines, established connections, associations, and special-interest groups would suddenly be disrupted. It struck me that for a while, at least, the government could concentrate on governing the country, instead of answering the clamoring of special-interest groups. I saw that this was true for myself as well, regarding my established views. Only by "removing the capital," could the decadence of ingrown and stagnant thinking be corrected, for so long as this remained in place, any new approach would soon bog down and get lost. This image made it clear that I must be willing to put aside my previous definitions of how things "ought to be," and look to the essential, timeless, and Cosmic elements of relationships.

Doing this, I was guided to abandon many older views I held on relating. With an empty mind, I was shown entirely new perspectives that completely shattered my prejudices and assumptions. Accordingly, I have been liberated and expanded. A new order has emerged.

As I worked, thought, and meditated, realizations came, not only on how to love without damage to ourselves, but on how to love with a great and good effect on others. The clarity of the realizations was such that I knew that I was being guided correctly, and that there exists no other way to heal and renew society than to unblock our abilities to love.

I relate this partly to point out that to make real changes within oneself, it is necessary to open our minds to think in new terms. We need, willingly, to persevere through situations of a difficult nature, because it is not possible to learn about loving without loving, just as it is not possible to learn to swim unless we are willing to take our feet off the bottom. Without being exposed to risk, we will be unable to uncover the Cosmic truths that lie concealed within us.

The version of the *I Ching* I have referred to throughout this book is the classic *I Ching or Book of Changes*, the Richard Wilhelm translation rendered into English by Cary F. Baynes, and published by Princeton University Press.

It needs to be said that certain words used in this book have different meanings than in ordinary usage. Modesty, for example, means humility as continuous conscientiousness; and innocence means an unacculturated mind. I have used masculine pronouns throughout, for the sake of convenience. This usage is in no way meant to imply gender.

Carol K. Anthony
April, 1993

Introduction

As the title indicates, this book about love is drawn from principles found in the *I Ching*. That I have found such principles embedded in this ancient Chinese book of wisdom may come as a surprise, since love, as I have written about it in this book, has hardly achieved cultural recognition in China, even today. There is still an implicit taboo on thinking in terms of such love.

This contradiction exists because the *I Ching*, as an oracle system, is known to be about 5000 years old, yet its greatest influence occurred during the Confucian era of 2500 years ago, when it became the centerpiece of Confucian philosophy. Held in high esteem by Confucius and his followers, the *I Ching* came to be used officially to train mandarins in the ruling of the country, and to enable the ruler to harmonize his edicts and actions with the "way of heaven." Despite this sanctioned official use of the *I Ching*, street-corner "sages," skilled in its use as an oracle, were frequently consulted over love and relationship problems. Nor was love entirely suppressed by the culture. Despite the prevalent social taboo on love, Cyril Birch stated, in his anthology *Chinese Literature from Early Times to the 14th Century* (Grove Press, N.Y. 1965), that love was a recurring theme, "ranging from the pristine freshness of courtship in the *Book of Songs*, to the laments for love unrequited or betrayed in the *tz'u* poets." He adds, "Given the social demands of marriage among the educated class, one would not expect to find much celebration of conjugal love, though Yüan Chen's moving memorial to his wife...is a notable exception to this observation."

The *I Ching*, in fact, speaks very much of love, and in its common use today it is frequently consulted about love relationship problems. Even though it mentions the word love only three times, and even then only in the commentary texts (twice in Hex. 1, in the commentary on The Judgment, and once in Hex. 37, Line 5), this fact speaks more about the *I Ching*'s modesty than about a lack in its content. That is to say, it is entirely about love, but rarely uses the word. For example, in consulting it over time, one is struck by the fact that the *I Ching* always counsels to keep one's mind open in regard to others, to hold to their potential to do the right thing, and to not allow oneself to become impatient and alienated. This, it says, gives people the necessary time and space to return to what is true and good within themselves. This sort of counsel implies a high and beautiful kind of love.

The *I Ching*, of course, can be applied to every kind of relationship and situation. Most of the great Chinese commentaries on the *I Ching* repeat the view that it is complete in its ability to give counsel for every circumstance. In my experience, its counsel is chiefly to be applied to loving, not only in the broadest sense of keeping an open mind and heart, but also in the most personal, earthy, intimate sense of loving. It is my further view that the chief use and purpose of the *I Ching* is to help us reawaken our awareness of the ever-present Cosmic intelligence that expresses itself constantly through feelings of love, and that this awakening occurs and is maintained through our experience of personal love. Implied in "The Judgment" of Hex. 1 is the concept that we exist in, or are an emanation and continuation of, the greater Cosmic principle of love. The very first words of this section proclaim: "The Creative works sublime success...." Confucius says of this, "Great indeed is the generating power of the Creative; all beings owe their beginning to it. This power permeates all heaven." The word "success" that occurs so often in the declarations of good fortune throughout the *I Ching*, means that unity (with another, with the Cosmos, with one's true nature, etc.) has been achieved.

The first two hexagrams of the *I Ching* represent the two primal forces of the Creative and the Receptive. They are said, through their interaction, to "give rise to all things," and are called the "yang" and "yin" forces. They are represented in the classic yang-yin symbol as interlocked, as if in embrace, within the Cosmic circle or unity called "Tai Chi," which denotes wholeness. Not only are they interlocked, yang and yin are wholly equal, interdependent and interactive. As polarities they are not in opposition but are complementary to each other. The various interrelationships of these two primal forces make up the whole of the *I Ching*'s 64 hexagrams, or chapters.

Hexagram 3, Line 4, counsels those who receive it, to "strive for union." The image is that of a horse and wagon being unhitched. The hitched and thus operative horse and wagon represent elements, such as two partners, who are meant to work together to achieve something worthwhile for the welfare of the whole. The attainment of unity and harmony between people is regarded throughout the many lines of the *I Ching* as the goal of one's endeavors.

The "nutrition" that is mentioned in Hexs. 5 and 27, refers to love. Hexs. 8 and 13 reassure us that love is the legitimate goal to be sought after, and that we will achieve this goal if we will relate properly. By this is meant that the essential conditions of any fellowship—what is Cosmically fair and just—must be met for relationships to find an enduring basis. Hexs. 34, 7, and 9, in calling us to rid ourselves of decadent habits of mind which create disunity in relationships, apply to the love relationship. They apply, as well, to our relationship with the Cosmos. Hexs. 26 and 62 guide us through crises of misunderstanding that occur in relationships. Hex. 31, is subtitled "wooing," and concerns how the love relationship can be manifested. Hex. 37 concerns the loving relationships that exist within the family. It applies to any relationship in which two individuals have inner ties, as well. These ties are seen to exist between those who have a natural affinity, one with the other. Hex. 54 points out the dangers to relationships that come from temptations of the wrong sort, and to the importance of holding to our values. Hex. 44 is similar, spelling out the essential principles of "coming to meet another halfway." This phrase describes the equal reciprocity that is fundamental to successful relationships. The *I Ching*, then, it can be fairly said, is truly about love.

All these references point to the Cosmos as operating on principles different from those commonly thought. We can compare the Cosmic reality to a hidden picture within another, obvious picture. The hidden picture is the Cosmic Order that is presented throughout the *I Ching* as the system of harmony that underlies and ultimately determines all things. This is quite the opposite of the picture of the Cosmos and its workings that has been presented by the historical world. The historical "reality," which has been shaped by human ideas, has also shaped our thinking to conform to it, rather than to what the *I Ching* refers to as our inner sense of truth, which is a feeling sense. The effect has been to divorce our thinking from our feelings, and thus to lose contact with our inner sense of truth. Inasmuch as we relate to other people from institutionalized human morés, we isolate ourselves from our natural feeling relationship with them. The *I Ching* makes us aware that by acknowledging the value of our feelings, we are enabled to return to harmony with our true selves and thereby to reconnect with the torrent of blessings the Cosmos is always ready to give to the true self. The usefulness of the *I Ching* is in showing us how to return to this self, and how doing so makes our relationships meaningful. Once this hidden picture of the Cosmic reality comes into view, the superficiality of the obvious picture presented as historical reality turns out to be obviously false. This picture is replaced by the gleaming beauty of the Cosmic reality.

To understand and see this inner picture, it is helpful to understand the historical process by which the outer picture developed. A question which emerged during the writing of this book was: how have we departed so far from our true selves, and why is it so difficult to understand our true natures? Books from three different areas of research provided keys to this question, one archeological, one historical, and one historical/psychological. Maria Gimbuta's archeological research from digs all over Europe (see *The Civilization of the Goddess*, HarperSanFrancisco, 1991) showed that artifacts from the current 2,500 year long patriarchal era have depicted mainly war and strife, while the artifacts of the preceding 30,000 year long matriarchal era have depicted a mainly peaceful coexistence between people. Heide Göttner-Abendroth's historical research on ancient matriarchal cultures (see *The Goddess and Her Heros*, Anthony Publishing Company, 1995) demonstrated that because of the distorting effects upon the personalities of men and women caused by the patriarchal view of life, it is impossible for us to know today what constitutes our true natures as men and women. That is to say, our attitudes about masculinity and femininity need to be seen as the result of this historical process, and not, as we may have assumed, as the way we really are. Jutta Voss, cleric and Jungian psychotherapist, wrote that the competition which now exists between the sexes is the result of this history, and contrary to our biological natures (see Das Schwarzmond-Tabu, Kreuz Verlag, 1988.

In the intervening years since 1993, when this book was first written, I learned that what psychoanalyst Karen Horney described as the "neurotic pride system," is nearly identical to the ego as I have come to understand it through working with the *I Ching*. Her observations coincide with mine especially as she sees this pride system not as an part of the person's true nature, but something that is the result of societal conditioning. (See her book, *The Struggle Toward Self-Realization, Neurosis and Human Growth*, W.W. Norton & Co., 1950.) These views, it needs also to be noted, coincide with those of Lao Tzu (see *Tao Te Ching*, trans. by Dr. John C. H. Wu., Shambala.)

More and more, since 1993, I have come to see the aberrations caused by patriarchy to be secondary to the much larger mindset that created it, and its vertical hierarchical thinking: the feudal mindset that has dominated most of the world for the last 3,000 years. If we think this mindset is limited to ancient cultures, which are mirrored in parts of the classic I Ching text and commentaries, we are mistaken. We do not shake off so easily its many presumptions that pervade our thinking. The system by which the individual's authorization of his own existence is mirrored in every social institution of our democratic societies, too. We are born in that matrix and we never think to question that it might be the principle reason why our most loving relationships fail.

Insofar as the institutionalized ideas damage the love relationship, they are mentioned in this book. To free ourselves from their damaging effects, we need to understand how they work against our true natures. The *I Ching*, with its patriarchal overlay, on the one hand, and its ability to call us back to our true natures, on the other, was the means by which these two pictures were made visible.

Chapter 1

The Inner Life of the Heart

This book is about love, what it is, and its Cosmic purpose in our lives. It is based on the premise that loving another is the single most important experience we shall have—the only experience that is capable of involving us deeply and completely on all levels of our being. It is about love as the essential harmonic of the Cosmos, the energy that drives our very existence, that when we allow it into our lives, to act upon us as it will, gives our life in a body meaning and brings it to completion.

The subject of love includes, as well, its dynamics as an energy and consciousness: what many people recognize as its psychic and physical aspects. It includes, as well, the problems and pitfalls that accompany loving another, and being loved by him in return. It seeks, through understanding, to make it possible to resolve and correct the attitudes and ideas we harbor that create these problems and pitfalls.

It would seem that there exist for us two major questions in life: whether we will allow the force of love in ourselves, along with all its dynamics, or whether we will allow the twin forces of doubt and fear, with their dynamics, to dominate. These forces are not passive. Once we allow them in, they will have their way with us, creating their own reality, the one positive and unifying, the other negative and dividing. The choice is entirely ours to make, free-willingly.

It needs to be added that this book is not about marriage or social convention. It makes no attempt to justify or not to justify, to protect or not to protect, what already exists in the way of social forms. It is, rather, about attitudes that create or destroy love, that affirm or deny the priority of the love relationship, that free or block our ability to love, and that enable or prevent us from answering the challenges10 of loving.

There exists a common superstition against subjecting love to close scrutiny. It is believed that examining love will somehow ruin it as an experience. Since so many love relationships fail, it seems clear we need thoroughly to scrutinize the love relationship.

Today's way of viewing relationships stems from the last 2500 years of patriarchal control of intimate relationships (see Introduction). Force, either in its outright physical form, or as the subtle force of tradition, still controls whom people can marry throughout much of the world. Only within the past 100 years in the West has there been relatively free choice in choosing a mate. Even then, the older views in which the main concerns were whether the match was good in terms of family, economics, and social connections, carried much more weight than whether relationships were based on, or had anything to do with, love. Old patriarchal attitudes in which one of the partners is expected to dominate and the other to yield, remain deeply seated, continuing to interject themselves harmfully into the love relationship. Furthermore, we lack models that show how two people in love can actualize and make their love endure within the context of freedom.

In this book, the *I Ching* (that ancient Chinese book of wisdom) has been the basis for scrutinizing the love relationship, because the *I Ching* has the unique capacity, when consulted, to mirror our innermost thoughts regarding the situations in which we are involved. It reflects back to us what we know intuitively to be true about these situations, reinforcing our inner knowledge of the way things work from the Cosmic standpoint. In the experience of this writer, it does this so much better and more accurately than any knowledge we can gain through purely external observation and logical analysis. The principles of conduct imbedded in the *I Ching* reflect the great harmonic that the Chinese call the "Tao," that means pragmatically, "the way the Cosmos works." Through this mirroring, we finally recognize that the Tao is love. This is expressed in the individual relationship as a deep inner connectedness.

The *I Ching* further makes us aware of the hidden power of our thoughts, both for good and evil. It is written throughout the *I Ching* that our secret, innermost thoughts subconsciously communicate to those with whom we have inner connections. In the love relationship, this effect is immediate and direct. If we can properly understand this hidden power for good and evil, we will be able to keep in harmony with the way nature works, and thereby build and keep vitally alive the all-important love relationship in our lives.

In the classic Wilhelm/Baynes translation of the *I Ching*, these secret, innermost thoughts are spoken of as "the thinking of the heart." They are also spoken of as "inner truth." Inner truth, however, has an extra dimension. It is our innate knowledge of the correct way. Great indeed, therefore, is the power of inner truth when we access it consciously, for then its power multiplies. Greater still is inner truth when we consciously embrace it, for it is then fully empowered by the force of the wholly united self.

In the love relationship, the lovers' innermost thoughts are immediately communicated to each other. They perceive these thoughts unconsciously, and react according to the way these perceptions make them feel. Thus, for example, if one has allowed himself to indulge in small critical thoughts about his beloved, he will then begin to feel slightly alienated. The beloved will immediately feel this beginning alienation and react accordingly, without even understanding why he is doing so.

To understand the nature of this interaction, it is necessary to understand the nature of our conscious (outer) self, and unconscious (inner) self. In the baby, these conscious and unconscious selves are one and the same and are experienced as a whole self. This unified self is primarily a feeling self that remains unified until, through its unique power of decision, it decides to accept abstract ideas that are in fundamental disagreement with what it knows and feels within. It does this upon the introduction of fears that cause the self to doubt what it knows. This doubt splits the personality into these two consciousnesses, or selves. Although the inner self continues to be all-knowing, it is suppressed so long as the doubts remain. Control of the personality is turned over to the outer self, which then goes on to construct ways of dealing with the doubts. It is at this point that the two begin to live separate lives.

This separation is not total, but exists only in those areas where doubt exists. Where doubt has not been aroused, we continue to respond to circumstances from our original, innocent self in a spontaneous, wholly adequate way.

It is important to realize that all doubts, and the way the outer self deals with them, create conflict with the inner self. These conflicts create tensions that affect us adversely, causing us to lose our sense of well-being, leading even to ill health.

The more the inner self relies on the outer for its decision making, the stronger the latter becomes. In time, it can entirely suppress the inner self, so that we lose our center. This is dangerous, for then we are no longer in harmony with the protective and nourishing Tao upon which the inner self depends.

Even though the inner self becomes totally suppressed, it remains in fundamental accord with the Tao. Furthermore, everyone's inner self is connected by a sympathetic accord with all people's inner selves. This accord is directly accessed in the love situation. It can even be accessed in the lost person.

Just as through the power of decision the outer self becomes separated from the inner self, we have the power to renew ourselves by re-deciding these erroneous constructs, thus restoring wholeness. Everyone who has come back from alcoholism or drug addiction, or even serious illness, has found the way to restore his inner self, if not entirely to wholeness, at least to stabilization. The great Chinese philosopher, Lao Tzu, called this activity "returning to the uncarved block." It has been likened to peeling off the layers of an onion until one gets back to the original self. Doing so removes the tension of inner conflicts and stops their harmful effects. Doing so also creates the foundation for the love relationship so that it is capable of enduring.

A contemporary metaphor for renewing the self is contained in the computer. We erase defective programs, build bigger ram space in terms of heart and mind, clean out negative and harmful memories stored, and rebuild our desktops, meaning, we restructure the way we perceive situations and experiences.

This metaphor is useful because it mirrors the way our minds work, how if we allow even the tiniest feelings of negation about the one we love to drift into our subconscious, these feelings become institutionalized or programmed into our thinking and attitudes. Once so institutionalized, they act as an internal program that is capable of creating what the *I Ching* calls inner "wars and lawsuits" that can continue subconsciously between lovers for years. (See Hexs. 6, 7, 21.)

To change harmful institutionalized patterns and attitudes, it is first necessary to learn to listen within, to develop an awareness of our inner sense of truth. On first attempting this, one may not be able to hear within at all. Through practicing daily meditation, this ability, which we had in our youth, gradually returns. At the height of the development of the true self, one is constantly aware of and in touch with it. Such an accomplishment requires an active interest, time, and perseverance. One finds, through developing oneself, that the rectification of relationships will not be achieved by telling others what to do, but by following the path that is correct for oneself. Only thus can we influence others for the good. Others are then able to recognize the firmness and reliability of our inner directive that becomes for them a golden floor upon which they can rely, upon which they can fall back when their misguided enthusiasm for what is false becomes exhausted. The *I Ching* makes us aware that all problems in our relationships are the result of this lack of inner firmness about what is good and correct. These problems result from being carelessly inattentive, and from having not been sincerely and actively devoted to what is true and good within ourselves.

There is written into the *I Ching*, and into Chinese philosophy generally, that our inner thoughts and attitudes are not passive in their effects, but create reality. Thus, negative attitudes create negative consequences, and positive attitudes create positive consequences. This view is expressed in the well-known Taoist maxim, "Harm enters only where fear makes an opening," and in Hex. 32, Line 3, "if a man remains at the mercy of moods of hope or fear aroused by the outer world...such inconsistency invariably leads to distressing experiences." Likewise, Hex. 25 describes the positive consequences that come from a mind that is "natural and true, unshadowed by ulterior designs. For wherever conscious purpose is to be seen, there the truth and innocence of nature have been lost.... Unsullied innocence...leads [one] to do right with instinctive sureness," and "brings about supreme success...." Conscious purpose, we begin to see, originates in the doubt that we have no such power over our lives. It contains, as well, a much larger doubt about the way the Cosmos works, because of the implication that although we follow the good, it does no good. The Cosmos, it would seem, is indifferent about us. Conscious purpose, therefore, is an attempt to overmaster the evil consequences of doubt and fear, without recognizing that doubt and fear are responsible for the evil consequences.

Through becoming aware of and teaching ourselves to accept only harmonious thoughts, and through rejecting negative thoughts that offer themselves, we can change the patterns that operate in our external lives. If we further develop the courage to trust what is harmonious, and to relate to external events in all the ways that are true to our original natures, what we have feared will no longer threaten us. That which most fulfills us will come to us as the logical consequence of providing in ourselves the climate for its existence.

We can immediately think of Scrooge, in Dickens' *A Christmas Carol,* as an example of the effect of changing one's attitude. Once Scrooge's negative attitudes were transformed through his experiences, his new attitude had good effects on those around him. The fate that we create by negative attitudes is not a fate set in stone. We can alter free ourselves from our fates through correcting these attitudes and the false presumptions on which they are based. This involves a kind of mental rejection that reverses our original acceptance of the false ideas. To use the computer as an analogy, we zap the old program. Doing so is like reformatting the driver and enlarging our view (our ram memory) to see what lies beyond the frame of reference defined by our old and inadeqate programs. To be sure, conscientious and persistent work on ourselves is required. Even though the steps by which such changes are achieved are necessarily small, they nevertheless succeed and sometimes in a quite dramatic way. Sometimes, by removing one key false phrase, we turn a key in a lock that opens a long closed door. That long closed door, we soon see, is the prison cell that was created by the false idea, and that false idea was the key phrase that enabled the whole false program. Then we see that prisoner held inside, often for many years, was nothing less than our true selves. Since writing the first edition of this book, I have discovered that finding these keys and zapping them has also freed people from long-standing health problems and ailments.

Changing negative attitudes is not a question of fighting oneself, as in forcing oneself to stop smoking. It is rather a question of bringing to maturity faculties of the psyche and body already in us that are only waiting to be exercised and developed. Development of the true self is natural to life, something that we are meant to do. The *I Ching* calls it "giving actuality to what is potential." It is to realize the Tao that resides in us. It is to fulfill the Cosmic image, or blueprint, that we carry with us.

Defective habits of mind, we need to realize, achieve power primarily because they are based on half-truths that have served as crutches for our personalities. Often we continue to lean on them simply because we have not realized we don't need them. Freeing ourselves from such crutches happens automatically as we grow stronger through perceiving the greater perspectives that set us free.

People do wrong or make mistakes almost entirely because they lack crucial insights into how things really work. They cheat, for example, because they distrust and fear that by following their natural inclination toward the good, they will attain their basic needs. Once they see with clarity that following the good is the only path leading to true happiness, they are able to discard the weakness of the old view. What brings them to this clarity are the inevitable dead-ends they reach through following fear- and doubt-driven paths. If at such points of crisis they can attain enough humility to ask within themselves for help, the Cosmos comes to their assistance. Finding the right way happens only when one has attained such humility.

Changes in ourselves are made easier when we recognize that what is required is not becoming something we are not, but rather freeing ourselves to be what we really are. Growth and transformation is always a question of seeking out and freeing ourselves from ideas and beliefs that are in conflict with our true natures and inner sense of truth. Growth and transformation, therefore, is a process of shedding what is false, disharmonious, and burdensome. It is a process that liberates us from misanthropy and alienation, and leads us from the darkness of negation into the light of love.

The inner life of the heart, where our innermost thoughts take place, exists for the most part on the unconscious plane. These thoughts, which are often perceptible only in quietly spoken, back-of-the-mind thoughts and observations, are reflected in our moods and attitudes, and in words that seem to come involuntarily out of our mouths. When, for example, due to a previous experience, we have concluded that "relationships are full of traps," suspicion and doubt will govern our relationships until we bring that thought into full consciousness and reject it. The smallest particle of doubt remaining from such a belief removes us from the harmless, absolute neutrality of an open mind. The doubts related to such underlying beliefs are not to be confused with natural feelings of caution that may arise when we sense something unsavory going on in another person's thoughts. These feelings, which are our natural first "early warnings" of the presence of conflicting elements in the other, need to be heeded.

The *I Ching* likens a harmonious, peaceful inner mind to the mirrored surface of a lake. This, too, is an image of trust. Conflict and doubt invariably roil the water up. The ripples that are initiated by partial doubt are as destructive as absolute doubt. If we wonder, for instance, whether a child is telling the truth about whether it stole something, simply holding that child in doubt until the facts are proven is to think that the child actually has stolen the thing. In a similar way, a previous love relationship that turned out badly will be the source of doubts when the prospect of being open once more to loving occurs. Inner barricades to loving often exist outside our conscious awareness, preventing us from admitting feelings of love when they do occur. Through meditation and work at developing our true self, it is possible to get in touch with such harmful attitudes, and to deprogram them. In doing this, we regain the childlike innocence of our original mind that is necessary to be able to love another.

Even though we can get in touch with these hidden and semi-hidden negative attitudes, it takes a long time to know our inner self entirely. Only gradually, through mirroring aids such as the *I Ching*, are we able to gain access to our innermost thoughts. Such mirroring occurs in the love relationship, where there is a need and drive to get in touch with one's innermost feelings. The love experience, if we will allow it when it comes, is the most powerful means by which we can get to know and develop ourselves. Because love touches us so deeply, because each partner is aware of and in love only with the other's true self, both are able to be mirrors for each other. Such mirroring can be said to be the main Cosmic function of the love relationship, for without it we cannot bring to actuality the true self within. Furthermore, if we are to make the love relationship endure, such mirroring, and the reflection and introspection it brings, is essential.

Chapter 2

The True Self and the Love Relationship

Immediately upon the beginning of a true love relationship, a dynamic connection is established between the two lover's innermost selves. This connection exists in the form of an energy that flows back and forth between them, binding them together. It is as if a large underground tunnel, through which blissful nourishment flows, connects them. They are able to feel this nourishment though they be thousands of miles apart.

Once activated, everything one feels is simultaneously felt by the beloved through the inner channel. Although what is communicated is largely in the form of emanations and feelings, words which are associated with feelings are "heard" by those who are psychic. Hexagram 61, Line 2, of the *I Ching* refers to this in saying that words spoken in the quiet of one's room, and which perfectly express what comes from the depths of the heart, "meet with assent at a distance of more than a thousand miles."

Whenever either of the lovers doubts, distrusts, denies, or attempts to reject the validity of their inner bond, he becomes blocked from his inner connection with the beloved. Any form of doubt or fear obstructs the channel. Hexagram 47, Line 4, notes another phenomenon, namely, that the one doubting is no longer able to see the beloved's face in his mind's eye. This sudden inability creates painful feelings of isolation and misery; nor is he any longer able to receive the nourishment that comes through the inner channel. When he returns to his true self by removing the obstructions, the loving contact returns. The more true a person is able to be to his innermost feelings, the more vibrantly the inner connection is felt and experienced.

The inner connection is also experienced as mutual attraction. Each feels the beloved to be like no one else he has ever known, and this is combined with an intuition that they share a destiny. If they are psychically aware, they consciously recognize that they belong to and complete each other. They often feel they have been connected in this way forever. During the beginning period of relationships, which the *I Ching* calls "difficulty at the beginning," the strength of these inner feelings helps to hold them together while their doubts and hesitations are being resolved.

The mutuality and intensity of their initial attraction differentiates true love from a one-sided infatuation. The true love relationship is marked by the dynamism that accompanies their instant recognition of each other. This often occurs through the eyes, in an instant and simultaneous recognition on first sight, but it can also happen audibly, on the telephone, or even in correspondence, when the way the other "is," in his inner self, becomes communicated and acknowledged on the unconscious plane before it emerges into consciousness. As a popular song describes it, friends awake one day to find that they are lovers. Regardless of how love awakens in the conscious mind, the lovers feel strongly that the Cosmos itself has arranged their coming together by a variety of bizarre and seemingly unrelated events. Then they find, to their surprise, that this vibrant inner channel has opened up between them. Often they feel there have been ancient ties of having been separated and now reunited. Such recognition comes from our deepest inner sense of truth.

The communications that go through the inner connection do so synchronously. Confucius described this inner accord as, "my heart in sympathy with yours." Doubts in one are felt and understood as such by the other. A cool, misanthropic attitude in one is felt by the other. Trust is felt likewise as trust, as are resistances and objections. Both, on this inner level, know and respond to the other's attitudes and feelings.

That we are able to communicate in this way is not surprising if we watch the way a flock of pigeons flies and recognize how inner communicating happens every day in the world around us. No doubt it is how human beings communicated before they developed speech.

Like the innocent babe, the love relationship is thrust into an organized society where "shoulds" and orchestrated responses have long governed relationships. As the depth and strength of their inner connection pushes itself into consciousness, it is resisted by inhibitions and fears of risk. This opposition from the outer self, with its shoulds, is responsible for the sense of shock and unreality that accompanies the beginning of a love relationship. As this self senses the power and potentially uncontrollable nature of the connection, defenses and fears arise. The promise of the joys of love are countered immediately by awareness of the risks involved in commitment. Many factors determine whether a person answers to his logical mind or whether he decides to answer his inner sense of truth.

Nearly all major changes and crises in life initiate similar feelings of shock. This happens because the new circumstance suddenly brings to the surface frustrations, longing, and deep needs which we have put aside. Liberated from their hiding places, these needs now demand our conscious attention. It is as if an unknown inner self suddenly demands, "You must recognize me, because I am who you really are! If you do not, you will ruin everything that is really important to us!"

Sooner or later this self within, from whom we have become separated, must assert itself. If we continue to deny it, it will attempt to break into consciousness by one means or another, as by annoying wake-up dreams and similar disturbing calls from the inner psyche. Failing to heed such calls, we may experience unpleasant events which further warn us of the necessity to recognize the true inner self.

Because the potential to love and the success of the love relationship is so connected with the inner self, it is necessary to understand how we have lost contact with it.

The main reason for losing contact with the inner self is the conditioning process that brings us to adulthood. Little by little, as we are trained, and because the inner self has no way of standing up to pressures of surrounding peers, a false self is created which adopts, accepts, and conforms to the values and ideas of the surrounding family and society. These values and ideas, installed in the memory as inner "shoulds," become orchestrated responses to situations. The newly created "should self," which consists of a variety of self-images, takes over as the ruler of consciousness, even speaking in the psyche as "I." An imposter in the psyche, this self is referred to throughout this book as the ego.

The development of the ego coincides with learning language. Verbal images are introduced into our minds by adults and peers to steer or push us toward acceptable self-images. We accept these images out of the fear that if we are to continue receiving love from those around us, we must become something more, or different from who we are.

Once we have adopted a successful ego, society reflects back its approval in the form of recognition and rewards, i.e., we find employment and are given regular advances. Later, as loyal members of the church and state, we become enforcers of the order, keepers and guardians of the acceptable image models. Finding our place in the established order, we then become part of the collective ego, regarding those who do not similarly conform with self-righteous anger. There is envy and vanity in the thought, "I have disciplined myself, how dare they not do it too!"

The collective ego is instantly aware of anyone who does not fit. Elements of wildness, of not having been appropriately tamed, inspire alarm. Artists and creative people who escape total domination by this process, often feel forced to create their own societies and stay aloof from those with conformist values. Most of us, on growing up, perceive this state of affairs in the social order and adjust our minds accordingly. We play the game, or else join groups of people with whom we can identify, to feel some sense of belonging, but even in these groups there will be tyranny in the form of a group-enforced standard. Having been trained to fear being isolated, we are held slavishly to conformity.

In the process of turning over direction of our lives in this way to the ego, the true self becomes repressed. Later, when we discover that the leadership of the ego is dangerous and destructive to the true interests of the self, the true self has an opportunity to reclaim the inner throne. At whatever point this happens, we find that the true self has remained precisely at the age where its development was halted years before—a child whose doubts about itself have not been resolved. But it has, at least, learned how dubious it is to easily and carelessly turn leadership of the personality back over to the ego. At this point, development of the true self can begin. Generally, development of the true self starts after shock and loss have impressed upon us the need to understand ourselves.

The ego, we learn, is not the true self, nor can it ever be. It is destined to be only the set of self-images we have chosen. It remains a role, or charade which is acted out daily with nearly total conviction. The desire and need of the inhibited true self to see the adopted self-images succeed, comes from the gnawing doubt that it has accepted about itself and its ability to lead the personality. The true self has invested its faith in the ego with the idea that if it believes in the ego's image enough, it will become real. Indeed, this investment is such that the image becomes real, and once it takes over, the ego begins to have its own way. To do this, it must keep the true self suppressed and imprisoned. This situation is felt subjectively as if we put on a dress or suit of clothes only to find that it has danced off with us in it, out of control. It can succeed in this powerful way to dominate our personality only so long as we believe its protestations that it is what it pretends to be: oneself.

Even though we feel the ego, and the rationales that justify it, to be real, the inner conflict continues within us, for never can we really fool ourselves. The inescapable truth is ever there, although suppressed. So long as the ego appears to be successful in managing things, this conflict remains out of sight, but the instant there is failure and shock, the conflict boils out into consciousness. The true self then regains control, at least until the ego manages to reassert that it has a new and better plan for success. If we only consider this rationale for an instant, the ego regains control.

Although the true love relationship can exist only between two people's true selves, relationships can exist between their egos. Such relationships are primarily pacts which promise, "I will support and further your ego if you support and further mine." Ego-based relationships are formed from logical choices that seem intelligent and affirm the self-image; but rather than adding to and building true self-esteem, these choices create a false, ego-based self-confidence in the partners' abilities to be clever and smart. Instead of liberating them to love so that the benefits spill over to everyone around them, their pacts isolate them from others, so that they must constantly be on guard against anything that might threaten their precarious balance. Lacking the inner strength of the true love relationship, ego-based relationships lack the trust that would free them from within, and the love that would fulfill their deepest, most fundamental needs.

Ego considerations can also invade the true love relationship. If not resisted, that relationship, too, will gradually be converted into an ego-based relationship, ending in the destruction of their love.

Only the energy of true love is capable of resonating between two people's true selves, thus supplying the vital *chi* energy that invigorates them and overflows to the world at large. When we settle for less than a true love relationship, nothing overflows, nothing rejuvenates. The couple remains starved for the barest emotional necessities. They end in carrying a heavy burden of repressed disappointment and anger, both at themselves and at the system which has convinced them to give up on being true to themselves.

Chapter 3

Love, A Cosmic Relationship

Love—the feeling that unites two people through an inner connection—can be recognized as originating in Cosmic love. This Cosmic love is like the endoplasm that surrounds the nucleus of a cell, from which the nucleus draws its nourishment in the form of proteins, and protection in the form of antibodies. We human beings are at all times surrounded and nourished by this love whether we are aware of it or not. As Lao Tzu put it:

"The Great Tao is universal like a flood.
How can it be turned to the right or to the left?
All creatures depend on it,
And it denies nothing to anyone.

It does its work,
But it makes no claims for itself."

To receive Cosmic love, we need only be open to it in the same way that the wall of the nucleus of a cell is permeable, and thus receives nourishment from the endoplasm. Openness, receptivity, and permeability enable the nourishment to flow freely into us, so that we absorb all that we need for our well-being. This nourishment is felt, once we are fully open to it, as bliss, and it infuses us with healthful invigorated feelings. These feelings are the same that we get on waking up to a gorgeous spring day filled with bird song after days of rain and gloom; it is a time, despite external circumstances, when one cannot help but notice how glorious it is to be alive.

Cosmic love pours into us like sunshine. There is no limit to our ability to receive it, so long as we remain open to it. We shut it off only when we allow negation and alienation in our thinking. We shut off Cosmic love, for example, when we question the worth or justice of our lives, and when we allow ourselves to fall into self-pity and envious comparisons. As we allow our openness to Cosmic love to shrink in this way, the nourishment that we depend on for *chi* energy shrinks accordingly. A hopeless attitude isolates us almost entirely from this necessary nourishment, thus we hear the expression of being in the "darkness of despair." If we allow our hearts to close completely, we relinquish the empowerment of our existence, for love is the all-empowering force.

Love is the great Cosmic energy. We can connect with it or not. It is always there, free to receive and to share with others, like sunshine. As an energy, it cannot be bottled up, saved, or hoarded. It can only flow into us, fill us up, and pass on. There is no such thing as love as a static thing that can be possessed. There is only loving, the active state of mind in which we are open, permeable, and dependent on the Cosmos.

The love relationship, originating in Cosmic love, is a Cosmic gift. This is implied in many hexagrams and lines of the *I Ching*. It is included, for example, in the overall meaning of Hex.19. Line 2 of this hexagram speaks of "the stimulus to approach" as "coming from a high place." This is similar to Hex. 54, Line 5, which says, "The emperor...gives his daughter in marriage when he sees fit." Such lines, in their metaphorical language, point out that intimate relationships are governed by the Cosmos. It is important, therefore, that the lovers recognize their dependence upon the Cosmos, because the love relationship is a three-way circuit that includes it. Maintaining their permeability and openness to each other, while remaining dependent on the Cosmos, keeps the lovers' relationship healthy and complete. If either shuts down his openness, or forgets his dependence upon, and responsibility to the Cosmos, his channel to the other becomes obstructed and the flow of nourishment becomes shut off. Alienation, negativism, doubt, and hopelessness, all subtle forms of resistance to the Cosmos, keep the lovers isolated from each other, inhibiting the pouring in of Cosmic love.

This view of Cosmic love is similar to the classical Chinese view of the nature of the Cosmos in which the positive interaction of the primal forces of yang and yin bring about the creation of all things. Through their harmonious interaction within the greater primal unity called Tai Chi, the Cosmic circuit of energy that creates life is made possible. This interaction is symbolized by the classic yang/yin symbol, in which yang and yin are unified in a Cosmic embrace.

The heart is the primary organ through which we perceive, receive, and transmit love. Our minds can imagine love but not feel it. We feel love in our hearts. Two lovers also feel love sexually, for in the close relationship in which two are united in love, their sexuality gives expression to their love, and is experienced as joyful bliss. Waiting for the "right time" to express this earthly aspect of love, and the nourishment it gives, is an important principle of the *I Ching* that shall be described in subsequent chapters.

Because of the way we grow up and learn to protect ourselves, we often become unable to receive and transmit love. We block our permeability to Cosmic love, and prevent the openness that is necessary to receive it as a gift. Fear and doubt, hurts and disappointments, cause us to distrust that love exists, therefore keep it from happening. It is natural to be interested in and to want love, the way a plant orients itself toward the light, but we are trained to be afraid of the necessary openness and trust that enable love. Negative relationships give rise to barricading the heart. Or, if we are open to love, the ego's attempts to secure the love relationship damages it. We grow up with such unnatural views of sexuality that pure and simple sexual expressions of love are made impossible. To be free enough to love, it is essential to deal with the ego and its destructive influence.

The love experience begins when the two are permitted to see, through the intervention of the Cosmos, the other's pure and good true selves. Each is permitted to see that the other is his natural and true mate. With this perception comes the knowledge that they fit together in their psychic and physical makeup like a key fitting into a lock. The grooves and spaces of the key and the lock fit precisely. They recognize that they need each other for their mutual growth and flowering, and that together they are able to develop strength and usefulness in the greater scheme of things beyond what either could achieve alone. That they are all these things to each other is due to their exact complementarity, and their inner perception of it motivates them to welcome each other into their inner spaces.

Because the love energy originates in the Cosmos, the lovers feel their meeting on the physical plane to be a completeness. This feeling of completeness gives love its joyful, tender, and passionate physical expression.

Not only does love come as a gift from the Cosmos, it nearly always comes as a surprise. This surprise creates doubt and the threat of rejection, but once the lovers get over this initial shock, they are able to recognize that they are truly the right ones for each other. In the meantime, however, both may fluctuate between acceptance and rejection until their true feelings break through. If only one of them rejects their bond in this way, the work of loving becomes very difficult for the other who has recognized and accepted it.

The time required to resolve such problems is called "the difficulty at the beginning." This period allows the residual doubts and fears that would damage the lovers' relationship, to be worked through. If they endure through this time in a constructive way, their fears will be replaced by a gradual building up of mutual trust that liberates the lovers' true selves. This liberation, in turn, manifests in the full flowering and externalizing of their love.

Chapter 4

The Predicament of the Loving Heart

Everyone is born with an open heart, ready to give and receive love. This is our natural true state. Very soon in life, however, the love we first receive as infants begins to be given and withheld intentionally by our parents as reward or punishment. Society does this, again, to make us conform to its requirements. Consequently, little by little, we forget what it means to have love without conditions attached, or that is not used to make us behave in a certain way. By the time we are old enough to form intimate relationships, it is no longer possible to love in a natural and innocent way.

The child is soon taught how, "for his own good," he should be insensitive to others, and how he should barricade himself from being hurt. He further learns to simulate love in the form of pretended affection and flattery, to be accepted and to gain selfish ends. Thus love becomes, in his mind, something to be used to get what he wants. Through the development of his ego, the child becomes further isolated from the innocently loving person that he was originally, and thus becomes insulated from any true love of others.

The barriers that result from this development make any meaningful relationship difficult, and the painful disappointments that result only further increase distrust. Becoming ever more isolated and rigidified, our hearts, as it were, become enclosed within an iron maiden that keeps others out and suffocates us from within.

Eventually, through grasping love selfishly and returning it only when absolutely necessary, even the little bit of love that comes to us soon disappears. Through repeating this isolating process over and over, people lose contact with their true selves altogether, and become hardened, hollow, egocentric, and vacant ego creatures, unable to care for others. This hollowness and alienation from the true self is experienced as a lack of self-worth that constantly needs the recognition, justification, and verification of others. This need is so oppressive that it drives many to drugs and alcohol, or to endless diversion in entertainment, or to constantly making their presence felt, by whatever means. To fulfill such needs, people pay attention to everyone else's business but their own, or look everywhere but within themselves for the causes of their troubles. This hollowness is the source of envy, greed, self-righteousness, and feelings of aggression.

Nearly all social decadence has its roots in this process by which people lose their true selves and end up with shut-off hearts. Drug dealers, whose business it is to offer substitutes for true nourishment, are quick to recognize people's unsatisfied longing.

In spite of the prevalence of such decadent influences, there always survive those who are able to keep their hearts open and loving. By some miracle they remain able to love without losing themselves in the process. These people seem to be able to develop the inner balance that enables them to continually enrich the lives of those around them. One recognizes in them that they possess the grace of being able to see good in everyone, and to cling to this good as potential, regardless of what shows in their external behavior. Such individuals seem to recognize that others' negative characteristics are only a charade that conceals their true selves. Alan Watts described this ability as the chief quality of the true guru, whose job, he said, is to awaken you to your true self, when you are ready to be awakened. When your ego is active, the guru says, in effect, "That is not you," and when your true self surfaces he says, with love and kindness, "Ah, that is really you."

There are still others who love openly, but to their harm. They fail to discriminate that the love they give to another's ego is the throwaway of self suggested in Hex. 64, Line 6, as "drunken love."

Contrary to popular belief, love is not to be given unconditionally, but only when the other is sincere, sensitive, and just. Its Cosmic purpose is to add to the growth and development of the beloved's true self, not to flatter and develop the ego.

The energy or impulse to love is a free-flowing energy to extend kindness and generosity to the beloved, as well as to others farther afield. If this energy is not to become exhausted, it must meet with reciprocity, so that love completes a circuit. Then the energy is constantly renewed. The reciprocity must be equal for this to happen, otherwise the energy drains off, becomes exhausted, and dies. To love and be loved, in the intimate relationship, is to be healthy and complete, each in himself. This completed energy circuit is similar to the human body cell, which, when healthy, has a completed and self-contained electrical circuit. Unhealthy cells, such as cancer cells, have interrupted, incomplete electrical circuits. The giving and receiving of love is the highest form of such energy circuits.

Because true love exists only between two people's true selves, there already is a complete and constant reciprocity on the inner level, even though it may not be consciously apparent to either. This inner relationship is secure, in and of itself, therefore there needs to be no search for security. Their approval of each other is complete, therefore there is no need to be recognized and valued, and no need for any orchestrated responses. Nor is there any need for either to exercise any degree of conscious effort on this level of relating. All their relating is spontaneous and intrinsic.

Outwardly, however, reciprocity exists only when both egos are displaced, and this may not always be the case. It is necessary, therefore, that the way one relates to the other be dependent on whether his ego is present and active, or absent, as there can be no true relationship between one's true self and another's ego. Whenever we give ourselves in an open loving way to the other while his ego is in control, we throw ourselves away and damage our self-esteem. It is the nature of the ego to always seek ways of dominating and interfering in the love relationship. It is necessary, therefore, to keep aware of both egos, so that when they appear, one's response is appropriate. If the other, for example, is insensitive, failure to note this fact and retreat from an open warmness sends his ego the message that such behavior is acceptable, and will be rewarded.

Retreat, it needs to be noted, is not meant to be a closure of the heart. It is rather a retreat from warmth and loving to an inner neutrality, where one remains until the other returns to sincerity and openness. If one has allowed the heart to close, reopening it requires a conscious decision that, when made, frees love's energy to once more flow outward. Failure to reopen the heart when the other is sincere and open damages the relationship.

Wise loving means responding according to the degree of reciprocity offered. It requires tuning one's awareness to where the other "is." When the other relates with sensitivity and sincerity, we are free to go forward to meet him. This assumes, of course, that we, too, are sensitive and sincere. This awareness is such that at the slightest hint of change that tells us the other is opening or closing, we open or close accordingly. (See Hex. 55, Lines 1-6.) This is the reciprocity that is necessary to create the environment in which love can be expressed safely, and in a mutually healthy way. In the *I Ching*, this principle is called "coming to meet halfway." (Hex. 44)

In this regard, it is necessary to distinguish between sincerity and orchestrated responses. We are taught to show love, kindness, and consideration, as good manners, social grace, and a means to success. We learn to expect others to perform these social graces in relating to us. The ego expects this in the love situation. Such orchestrated responses, however, are not the sincerity and sensitivity referred to here, that come from the inner self. The orchestrated response is mixed up with intention, and a desire to control the situation for the ego's benefit. Performing in this way obscures true feelings. Expecting others to perform similarly keeps us from understanding their true feelings. Because it is against the lover's inner dignity to perform according to his beloved's ego expectations, many of the misunderstandings lovers have revolve around this issue. Lovers can give the gifts of love freely only when the beloved does not wait with his hand out in expectation, or in the chiding stance, "You ought to...."

Given the way we are brought up, a true reciprocity is not immediately possible in many relationships. This is because the patriarchal tradition has prohibited the true equality that must exist between partners in love. Interestingly, during the mating period preceding ordinary marriages, there is no presumption of a hierarchy in the relationship. Often the opposite happens after marriage. Until very recently, it was the common law in the United States that women "owed" it to their husbands to submit to their sexual demands; failure to do so could cause the woman to lose her rights in a divorce. Although this situation may no longer legally exist, the attitude that people have such rights still exists. Such attitudes destroy the spontaneity and equality that is essential to the free-willed love relationship.

Equality is also necessary to the environment in which love can be safely expressed, otherwise the one who gives too much becomes exhausted, while the one receiving without giving becomes sated and restless. Wise loving requires that we observe these and other elements essential to love. Failure to do so will interfere with or even destroy love.

If the lovers rush into the relationship before certain reservations of attitude have been allowed to surface and be dealt with, the trust that is necessary to the environment of love will remain incomplete. (Hex. 53.) Deeply rooted trust comes from a slow maturing of inner feelings. Superficial trust will contain hidden, "Let's see" elements that imply that if things do not go well, one can back out. When trust is incomplete, both remain on guard and their suspicions block the sincere effort both need to put into the development of their relationship.

Those who love indiscriminately, rush into intimacy repeatedly before a safe environment for love has been established. They do this believing that their love will be strong enough to bear all burdens, such as the other's doubts and burnout generated by previous relationships. Also, ego elements that have not been disciplined surface in intense struggles for dominance.

When one of a couple manages to dominate, the couple is prevented from attaining the humility that deepens their love and secures it on the inner plane. Like all alive growing things, love has a natural progression and development that leads to maturation. If this progression is neglected or bypassed, inequality and injustice will characterize the relationship. Then neither of the lovers will be able to complete the development of their true selves that love is meant to serve. The gift of love carries with it the Cosmic responsibility to love correctly, and that is why failing to do so creates suffering.

Loving wisely, then, means that it is necessary for lovers to approach each other carefully and conscientiously. The very beginning is the time when it is most possible to build this basis. The lovers will need to proceed carefully and thoughtfully, with neither catering to the other's ego, nor compromising on important principles. If they patiently see this time through to its completion, potential problems will gradually dissolve as trust grows. When this trust is complete, they will be able to open up to each other freely and safely.

Chapter 5

Difficulty at the Beginning

It goes without saying that people can be attracted to each other for many reasons. The sort of attraction that accompanies the establishment of an inner connection, however, occurs when two have perceived each other's true selves. This perception is accompanied by a joyful subconscious recognition that is often conscious as well. It manifests as an electrifying circuit of energy running between them that has the potential to draw them together in unity.

Each feels that the other alone has the ability to understand and value him as he really is. There is subconscious joy at being invited into the other's inner space. On the outer level, there is the prospect of sharing the novelty of the other's outlook, humor, sensitivity, and trust, and of the unfolding surprises that come with the other's differences. Each perceives that he will be expanded and challenged to grow to his fullest capacity. This array of new feelings and perceptions can be almost overwhelming.

Nearly all that one perceives, during this first awareness of love, is potential. What neither perceives is the tentativeness of the situation. While on the one hand the inner connection is strong, its strength is overmatched by the strength of their egos, that feel quite another set of feelings.

Their egos are caught unaware at first, due to the shock and suddenness with which the attachment and inner connection occurs. Shock always displaces the ego temporarily, because it is comprised, for the most part, of a set of orchestrated responses to a list of foreseeable situations. Situations that are outside its imagination or experience catch the ego unprepared, and it takes some time for it to identify, compare, and place the new experiences into its existing set of pigeonholes. Soon enough, however, the ego processes the greater part of this information into positive and negative categories. Into the positive category it thrusts every conceivable means by which it can be affirmed and fed, and into the negative category, every potential threat to its control. It sees the other in terms of giving himself selflessly and loyally in devotion to the partner, in terms of being able to dump its burdens onto the other, and in terms of being helped to achieve its ambition to succeed in life. The ego makes a balance sheet, putting the imagined benefits on one side, and the deficits on the other. If the deficits are very apparent, it will offer resistances.

This ego-centered looking and measuring on both parts is the source of many of the problems that occur in the beginning. As guardian of the pride system, the ego seeks to extend its dominance to take over control of the other. The difficulty at the beginning, therefore, centers around the disparity between the hopes and loving feelings of their true selves, on the one hand, and the demands of their egos, on the other. During this period, they are meant to dissolve the obstructions that their egos put up to the successful externalizing of their love. This work involves setting the limits that create the environment of love.

There is a need to put limits on ego-based fears. These fears are expressed in the *I Ching* in Hexagram 38, *Opposition*, a hexagram that describes the dangers of shutting off a person who seems to be opposite, but who in reality is complementary to one's own nature. This apparent opposition is the source of misunderstandings that make difficulties for partners with different viewpoints and temperaments. One may be more reserved, the other more outgoing, one may be more intellectual, the other more intuitive, one more studious, the other more physically active, one more disciplined in some things while the other is more disciplined in others. While these things create misunderstanding, when understood and resolved, the partners' differences make it possible for them to serve as mirrors for each other.

At first these misunderstandings are not evident, partly because the lovers are entirely beguiled by the images of each other's true selves. They have not yet differentiated that much of what they see is potential rather than actual. The blueprint of their true natures is as yet only a blueprint. Certainly, each will want to show the other only his best self. They will, for a time, be totally blind to the disuniting factors that are already in place. There are plenty of hints of these factors, but lovers, especially those who have had no experience of love, do not heed the warning signs. Soon enough, the ego of one or the other breaks out. This leads to their first quarrel, when they recognize that important hesitations that have been hidden or suppressed suddenly have a harsh reality.

For such reasons it is best that the lovers take the time, right at the beginning, to allow every hesitation and doubt to come up, to be put on the table and faced squarely. The problems one finds are not insuperable. We all have egos that must be dealt with. We need to examine not only the other's list of expectations and complaints, but ours as well, to be sure that what we require is truly just, and not merely what is expected in the way of orchestrated responses by society, friends, and family. Most importantly, we should not pretend that all is perfect, just to satisfy vanity.

During this time, both people's egos will engage in a struggle for dominance, with each challenging the other's ego. This activity may even advance to a state of warfare, a truly dangerous time for the lovers, when their wills will be challenged to give up on the relationship altogether. This must not be. It is important to recognize and accept this activity as part of the essential task of working through the difficulties at the beginning.

The answer lies not, as contemporary social morés and the patriarchal system suggest, in either one dominating, but in their coming to an understanding of the necessary limits that permit true unity. Submission of either only defeats the purpose of true love, which is to strengthen and develop both their true selves to the point where they can throw off the ego's leadership. This requires both to work at shrinking their ego's control.

Among the problems that characterize the difficulty at the beginning are certain hesitations that need to be worked through. Some of these are natural, some ego-induced. Human beings are naturally hesitant to welcome another into their intimate space. We intuitively recognize that in becoming intimate with another, we are opening ourselves up to aspects of our personality that are hidden from us. We seem to intuitively understand the boundaries of our psyche and know that if we go beyond them, we will suffer harm. These hesitations, therefore, are natural, similar to the hesitations small children have about accepting kisses from strangers.

A person's psyche is not unlike a kingdom. The intended ruler of the psyche is one's true self. While, during the early developmental years, the true self has turned parts of the psyche over to the leadership of the ego, there remain areas that are still controlled by the true self. If the parents have not been totally invasive into the child's deepest feelings, he will still be able to recognize what he truly feels, and be protective against anyone's further invasion into these areas. The true self, therefore, instinctively will resist allowing another's ego into this innermost space. This instinct will manifest as a certain hesitancy to come forward until he is sure that the other's ego will not encroach, or in any way threaten his inner balance. This hesitation is not an active distrust, but an attitude of caution.

In the true love relationship, each one's true self will naturally respect this area of the other's psyche, a respect which, if it is maintained, will develop a trust that, in time, will dissolve their hesitations. The individual ego, however, fears this hesitation in the other, and views the other's privacy and hesitation as a potential threat to its security. For this reason it will seek access into it, in order to control it. At first it will attempt to do this through flattery or persuasion, but more direct efforts to control will also be employed, such as threatening to withhold love, or giving up on the relationship.

We are also naturally shy to expose the most earthy physical aspects of ourselves unless there is humility, tenderness, and sensitivity on the part of the other. Acculturation, in the form of the entertainment media and much psychological theory, would encourage us to intentionally break down this natural barrier. When we do so, however, we betray and humiliate our true selves. This humiliation, which is commonly called "losing one's innocence," was the motive behind the custom of having the virgin young man visit the prostitute. It led to the desensitization that was necessary for the young man to carry on the patriarchal tradition of male dominance over the "inferior" female. This attitude remains the major cause of rape of women today.

This tradition continues through attempts to break down our natural inhibitions to sexual intimacy. At the same time, love is held as some sort of nonsense and craziness that no self-respecting person should take seriously. From the *I Ching* point of view, physical intimacy that is not accompanied by love goes against a person's true nature.

Premature intimacy in the love relationship, while not incorrect, can be the source of many difficulties if it occurs before these natural hesitations are dealt with. This is because premature sexuality represses one's natural hesitations. The resulting repression is always harmful to the psyche., rather than building up the necessary confidence in the love partners.

Giving oneself in intimacy, while trust, fairness, equality, reciprocity, and sensitivity are lacking or are not fully established, is to compromise the essentials of relating. It is what in the *I Ching* is called "throwing oneself away." (See Hex. 41, Lines 1 and 2.) This compromise exposes one's inner dignity and self-worth to feelings of degradation. It is to say, in effect,

"I will join you, even though we have not established a basis for relating," thus sacrificing dignity and self-respect in hopes of gaining nourishment. There is no gain to be made when one gives oneself to a robber (the ego). With the lowering of self-esteem, the true self feels more unworthy to govern the personality, therefore turns even more control over to the inept ego. The damage incurred from becoming intimate prematurely is not insuperable where there is true love, but every single step overleapt has its cost.

In addition to natural hesitations, each brings with him habits of mind, fears, expectations, hopes, and demands, and even areas of pain that the other cannot know about. Such negative experiences comprise a sort of burnout, or exhaustion of patience that exist as hidden elements and can surface unexpectedly under stress. The lover who is on the receiving end of such reactions will lack an adequate basis to understand them. He will feel hurt and begin to distrust the other, placing their love under even more stress.

Premature physical intimacy not only makes the resolution of such problems more difficult, the magnitude of the problems is increased by a fully awakened sexuality that is now subjected to doubt. The threats to the psyche grow much greater, sometimes leading to despair. Despair, in turn, creates vicious cycles that must be worked through. For such reasons, it is important not to rush into physical intimacy until serious hesitations and distrust have received our full attention, and are worked through.

The time of difficulty at the beginning is a time when the lovers prepare themselves for the new relationship. There are many chores they need to accomplish to make themselves ready and open to loving, if their love is to last. For example, part of their preparation may be to face and complete any unfinished business that exists in the form of previous love relationships. Subconsciously, these will have already concluded, otherwise the new relationship could not have begun, but this fact may not have registered consciously. Finishing this business means that the previous relationship must be brought to full consciousness, faced, and be allowed to reach its conclusion. Among such items may be inner pacts we have made to be faithful to another. Such pacts create a false sense of duty and guilt that causes one to hold back in the new relationship.

Getting to know one another requires time, and therefore a willingness to be patient. Each needs to see that every negative thing that happens is not directed at him personally. Most misunderstandings come from people's judging events and situations from preconceived points of view. For example, a person who has been involved in an unsuccessful previous relationship may constantly fear that the new beloved might have the same faults as the former. Such a person will be on the lookout for telltale signs of trouble, and therefore easily misinterpret this or that statement or action as evidence of what he most fears. Individuals who have been disappointed before, and who have not worked through these disappointments, may be so armed against failure that they are poised to quit before the other can quit first. Because love and trust are interdependent, distrust that is not allowed to dissipate through the building of trust, will almost certainly cause the relationship to fail later on.

Establishing love beyond the first tender but powerful attraction requires working through and dealing with material of this sort. Dealing with these issues entails building in oneself the precise qualities of character that are needed to make the relationship endure. Seeing this period through to its completion ends in the establishment of complete trust. Trust, we begin to see, is an inner acknowledgment of their bond. Throughout the patriarchal period, the bonding of a couple has meant legally promising one's mate numbers of things, and performing numerous orchestrated responses to make everything harmonious. Supporting these promises were the powerful forces of law, religion, and custom, hanging like swords over the head. The inner acknowledgment of the bond of true love is something that cannot be forced. It is something that happens, but only when each lover's firmness about what is correct and essential has won the other's trust. It is this trust that enables them to give themselves freely and completely. There is no need for external commitment, pacts, or promises.

Chapter 6

Coming to Meet Halfway

Coming to meet halfway is the *I Ching* metaphor for the natural ease and attraction that brings two people together in the love relationship (see Hex. 44). This ease and attraction is quite innocent and natural. There may not even be a hint of a love relationship, so that the fact steals upon them quite gradually. But it can also happen quite suddenly, when their eyes first meet, that they recognize the other as their love partner.

This meeting is quite different from a one-sided wishing for a relationship that invariably leads to humiliation. The *I Ching* says of this, in Hex. 4, Line 4, "For youthful folly it is the most hopeless thing to entangle itself in empty imagining. The more obstinately it clings to such unreal fantasies, the more certainly will humiliation overtake it. Often the teacher [the Sage that speaks through the *I Ching*] has no other course but to leave the fool to himself for a time, not sparing him the humiliation that results. This is frequently the only means of rescue."

Hexagram 44, following this principle, warns one not to accept someone who carelessly and easily offers himself. This does not mean that he is not suited, but that there will be a price to pay for skipping steps. Neither should run precipitously after the other, but allow the relationship to develop naturally.

Meeting halfway also points to the effort each makes, willingly, from his natural impulse to move toward the other, and to understand and respond sympathetically to him. Confucius spoke of this behavior as "my heart in sympathy with yours." Each has a heartfelt willingness to do his share in trying to be fair, just, and sensitive. It is the continuous conscientiousness that the *I Ching* calls modesty. This modesty is free of the careless indifference that makes one assume that the blessings of life are owed to one, or that one is free to say whatever comes to mind without sensitivity to where the other is, or without regard for his right to think for himself and to find his own way.

Meeting halfway applies both to the inner and the outer planes of relationships. Those who love automatically meet the other halfway on the inner plane. As they get to know the other and come into contact with each other's egos, complaints and hesitations cause doubts as to whether the beloved is truly the person one thought him to be in the beginning. Such doubts begin to close the aperture of the heart and are what Hex. 2, Line 1, calls "the first signs of hoarfrost turning to ice." Allowing one's thoughts of the beloved to cool in this way not only sends the beloved a negative message that increases his distrust, it also blocks one from feeling the love that comes through the inner channel. Once a lover has lost his connection with the other through allowing his feelings to cool, the connection can only be restored by reopening his heart and mind. This is done by disallowing any further negative thoughts, and asking the Cosmos for help to reopen the heart. There is often a lag in time before the other's presence is felt again, but the good effect of reopening oneself is immediate.

Meeting halfway also refers to the mating dance called wooing. It is the process by which the lovers move toward each other on the outer plane to bring their love to completion in unity. This process has natural steps that establish the limitations that apply to relationships. None of these steps can be skipped over, rushed, or avoided. Each step involves an important breakthrough in understanding how to relate.

Just as in business negotiations it is important to get all issues on the table prior to signing the contract, meeting halfway means that each brings into his own consciousness all hidden agendas, back-of-the-mind issues, and hidden reservations of attitude. The essence of a relationship is self-examination. In the absence of it, each will try to manipulate or ambush the other by unleashing stored-up grievances and making capricious requirements. Meeting halfway requires the lovers to view each other's mistakes and transgressions moderately, so that they do not allow their loving energies to cool. Moderation allows the one who has offended or erred the necessary space to return to being his true self. This extension of respect enables each to recognize how difficult it is to tame his own ego.

Meeting halfway also means that the lovers keep their inner connection with the other intact and interactive. This means they do not allow their feelings to degenerate into satiation, egotistical restlessness, or any measuring and comparing to see whether they have got the best out of life, or whether there are not greener fields farther away. They do not hold back the nourishment of their love when the other is open and sincere. As Hex. 37, Line 2, advises, they attend to nourishing the relationship; this is the lover's "great and important duty," which brings good fortune "to the whole house."

Nourishing the other on the inner level does not mean that the lovers consciously project thoughts of love to each other, but that they protect their natural warm and loving feelings from the cooling effects of complaints, faultfinding, feelings of hopelessness, fear, doubt, jealous imagining, envy, and similar negative thoughts that the *I Ching* calls "stagnating stuff" in Hex. 50, Line 1, and "spoiled food" in Hex. 18. Regardless of what the beloved is doing that seems contrary to unifying the relationship, it is important to see his true self as whole and good, and that he is the precisely correct person for the development of one's own true self. Seeing him this way nourishes and strengthens his inner self. Maintaining this inner loyalty is essential, regardless of how one may need to be reserved on the outer level.

The *I Ching* metaphor for our conscious mind is that of a container in which our thoughts are held. This "Ting," as it was called, was a three-legged vessel used in ancient China for making ceremonial sacrifices of cooked food to the gods. What we keep in our Ting, in the form of thoughts, is what we offer to the Cosmos as nourishment, good or bad. It is important, therefore, to be conscientious that one's thoughts always be good nourishment. Likewise, meeting halfway means the lovers love conscientiously, sacrificing negative and destructive thoughts that create doubt and resistance in the relationship. They hold only good thoughts that heal and help the relationship.

Encroachment

Encroachment, in the love relationship, happens when one of the lovers goes further than meeting the other halfway. Each of the lovers, initially, welcomes the other into his inner space. This happens on the unconscious plane, and sometimes on the conscious plane as well. Observing the principles of meeting halfway, however, they are never meant to become more than guests in the other's space. If they maintain a modest, cautious, and obliging attitude, and do not give themselves "airs," they can "acquire a home" in the other's heart, but they are ever like wanderers in a strange land, in that they must take care "to remain upright and steadfast," and "sojourn only in the proper places" (see Hex. 56). Any deviation from this modest attitude blocks them from their inner connection, and if continued, leads to alienation.

While it is true that the lovers belong to each other inwardly, this does not mean they own each other. They are not entitled to do what they please with each other. Such attitudes have no place in the free-willed love relationship. The inner response to such an attitude is a firm inner No. This prevents an inner war or lawsuit, which would block their ability to feel each other through the inner connection, and cause them both to feel miserable. The one encroaching will otherwise pay for this error through suffering a loss of pride and being humiliated. Loss of pride would then become a further complication if he is unable to retreat and correct himself.

Encroachment occurs on the outer level, for example, through presuming upon the other. This can be in a small or large way, as when one telephones at unusual and inconvenient hours on the assumption that it is one's privilege to do so. Or one gives the other advice that he has not wanted or sought. Even saying words such as, "I love you" when the other has not created an opening, can be an encroachment.

Wooing by flattery is another form of encroachment. When this fails to have the desired effect, the flatterer is humiliated. Intention, of any sort, such as using love as a means to advance oneself, as in marrying for money or position, is an encroachment that springs from the weakness of doubt and fear. Intention is also involved when the ego reasons, "If I don't do something, nothing will ever happen." In the love relationship, everything must be achieved on the inner level first, before it can become manifest on the outer level. Love cannot be bought, nor can it be gained through lavishing gifts, or by any device, contrivance, or orchestrated response. Such efforts originate in a distrust of their inner connection that the other feels and responds to with distrust (and also with contempt). This is not to say that gifts cannot be given, that friendliness is out of place, or that loving gestures are inappropriate. It is simply to say that the ego cannot use them successfully as a means to its ends. Whenever there is conscious intent, and contriving is present, the ego is active and will invariably fail in its devices.

Love is the opposite of encroachment; it is respecting one's own space and the other's; it is also to retreat when other fails to respect us. It is caring enough for our dignity not to go where not invited, and not to press ourselves on the other. It means that we extend trust to him, but we also to say an inner No and retreat when he abuses that trust. We trust that without our help or doing, he will develop the will to meet us halfway. We trust him to grow, and to understand, and become sensitive to us. We trust him to recognize his mistakes. We trust him to the extent that we do not watch over or mentally supervise him. Such trust manifests itself when we remain gentle but firm that he treat us with respect; and when, although we have been given every justification, we manage not to be condescending, disdainful, or harsh.

Advancing and Retreating with the Openings and Closings

On the outer level, lovers meet each other halfway when they are open and receptive. The rule is to respond only.

Responding requires being aware of the emanations that the other sends through the inner channel. This means being attuned to the small signs that tell us when the other is open and receptive. It means that we feel how open the other is at any given moment of contact. If the other has opened a door, we make sure whether it is opened wide enough to go through. We need to keep aware, to sense when the door opens further, or when it begins to close. We go with this movement.

Following this movement, it is necessary to recognize that every opening made by the other is conditional. While his true self may have opened the door half-way, his ego often stands just behind, watching both to protect itself, and to seize opportunities that might serve its purposes. We need to promptly retreat when the other's ego has entered the stage.

This kind of sensitivity and awareness builds trust between lovers. The more they relate to the other in this respectful manner, the more they trust and open up to each other. Conversely, when they ignore the small signs that tell when the other is closing the door, the other's trust diminishes.

Love as Simplicity

Love by its nature is simple. This simplicity provides the perfect model for what is meant by meeting halfway. One loves because it is one's nature to love. Love is expressed simply as caring. It cannot be contrived. The ego always strives, through employing orchestrated responses, to gain control, to obtain recognition, and to win unfair conditions. Its aim, invariably, is to dominate the relationship and have things its way.

It is right and correct that each do his share. Many otherwise good people, after putting themselves forward to establish a relationship, immediately sink back into convivial indolence and reciprocate as little as possible. It is incorrect to overlook such spoiled habits. The desire for things to always go smoothly, at any cost, ends in self-betrayal. It is part of the work of loving to step back into an attitude of reserve until the other does his share of relating. Doing his share means coming forward in sincerity, out of love, and not just doing what he thinks might be expected of him.

Meeting halfway means reciprocity, in that each must complete his half of the circuit of love energy. When a lover returns from being insensitive, it is important that the other meet him halfway, and not hang back sulkily. In these situations one needs to respond, not from orchestrated responses, but as the situation of the moment demands.

Despite one's efforts to relate correctly, sometimes it happens that the other continues to behave unjustly. In such cases, it is necessary to let the other go, and to go on with one's life. Doing this gives him the time and space he needs in order to have a breakthrough in his understanding. Loving is walking away in the trust that he will someday discover the truth for himself.

Strength in Relationships

Recently, a wife visiting a psychiatrist stated that she wanted her husband to be strong, saying that she felt they could not be "as one" until he showed strength. Further questioning showed that by strength she did not mean she wanted him to dominate her. She wanted gentleness and tenderness. She wanted to be the woman in his life, to have his love, but she also wanted him to have a sense of himself that there were things he would not do, even for her. She was saying that it was impossible to give herself wholly to him as long as he lacked a firm sense of direction and self-worth.

Each partner needs this kind of strength from the other. Strength means that a person has put limits on his ego. He is unwilling to cede to his partner his personal responsibility for his relationship to the Cosmos. He does not ignore what is correct, just to make things go smoothly. He is tenderly careful, but not out of fear of losing the other's love. He is considerate, but without abandoning self-respect. He does not invade or encroach. Most of all, he has an inner set of limits that do not permit him to take advantage of the other. He is patient, but will not be pushed around. He is his own master and best friend, therefore able to be true to himself. This kind of strength respects another's space.

Such a person never makes advances beyond those welcome. He retreats instantly when he feels the other to be hesitant, afraid, distrustful, or repulsed. He allows the other to deal with his fears and hesitancies, and he waits rather than sell his principles short.

This strength is self-leadership, an unwillingness to slip into apathy and decadence. This same strength enables a lover to wait until the other opens up to him; he does not need to rush the process, but allows the flowering to be completed in its own way, in its own time. He uses no strategy or arguments but simply, patiently, and in humility sees the process through.

There will always be the danger, once a relationship is

established, of one or both relaxing into egotism, the feeling that they somehow have won something. If this attitude is not corrected, it will, in time, collapse the trust that has been built. Similarly, ebullient egotism and dominance will awaken distrust and unrest. The biggest danger, therefore, is neglect, the careless abandonment of these principles. The strong person will remain disciplined and conscientious in his way of life.

Whether a person has this kind of inner strength is something people know about each other intuitively. It is never something that can be achieved by any kind of ego-led bravado. It must be real. Nor will either necessarily have developed it at the beginning of their relationship. It is something they develop through learning to relate to each other.

The person who becomes truly strong in this way earns the love, credibility, and respect he receives, because he has attained true leadership and command over himself. This kind of strength, therefore, is the necessary element that enables lovers to meet each other halfway.

Chapter 7

The Ego as the Enemy of Love

In the formation of the individual ego, we not only adopt images we hope will make our life successful, we hope, through acting out these images, to protect ourselves from being disapproved of and isolated by the collective ego. Psychoanalyst Karen Horney recognized the ego as an organized system of neurotic pride that we create to protect the personality from feelings of embarrassment and disappointment. She noted that once adopted, the ego tends to assert that it is the glorious person it pretends to be, and then acts to protect itself from being seen as otherwise. This permits the ego to criticize negative qualities in others that it obviously has in itself, without its noticing any contradiction. This aspect of the ego makes it difficult for us to know ourselves.

We are encouraged from an early age by those around us to adopt the idea that we are by nature inadequate to meet the emotional challenges of life, and that we need to develop an adequate response. This fear of inadequacy creates the need for the ego, and the feeling that we cannot get along without it. Therefore, we begin to rely on projected images of ourselves to overmaster, or deflect through bravado, what we fear.

Behaving as if we are something more than we truly are, we begin to isolate ourselves from living life and being able to love in the natural and true way that is in harmony with the Cosmos. (See Hex. 25.) Once we accept as true the rationales by which we transfer power to the ego, those same rationales are then used by the ego to remind us of why we "need" it, as a mechanism to maintain its control. Each and every time we begin to see that the ego is the enemy within, it subliminally reiterates these rationales, together with all the fears and doubts of self that have accompanied the ego's installation in the psyche.

Because of the need to constantly justify its existence, the ego continually focuses on how it protects us from risk, from the disapproval of others, and how it "knows the sure way to success." For this reason we have a society that is attached to earning more than enough, to acquiring tenure, to striving upward on the social, economic ladders, and so on, depending on the insecurity the ego most prevalently uses to keep the true self in submission. It is the reason people allow themselves to depend on hierarchical structures, and hang onto the coattails of friends who act in aggressive and powerful ways, and otherwise try to insulate themselves from the vagaries of chance. In this way, they never learn that the Cosmos is not only not hostile when we depend upon it, but that when we are in harmony with it, it helps us obtain everything we need.

Just as the ego searches for security in social life, it searches for security in love, therefore it is never anything but a destabilizing and untrustworthy element in the love relationship. Love is a free Cosmic gift that cannot be secured by any means.

The ego does not dominate every aspect of our personality, only those aspects that present risk to its pride system. No other relationship is as capable of destabilizing the false, but neat and orderly looking world of the ego as the love relationship, because its Cosmic purpose is to free the true self from the ego's dominance. On this account, the ego puts forth every effort to control the relationship by inserting itself into the place of dominance. The fears that prevent us from loving come from the ego, precisely because love is the one experience that allows us to grow and find fulfillment in our lives.

Not only is the self-assured, contriving, defensive ego an enemy of love, it is not capable of loving. For this reason, when confronted with another's ego in the love relationship, one must not mistake or accept it as the other's true self, for it is only a charade and imposter that claims to be the self. If one makes the mistake of catering to the beloved's ego, one aids that ego in keeping the other's true self repressed. Worse, one helps that ego gain dominance over the relationship. As it is put in Hex. 27, Line 2, the kinds of flattery that the ego would call love are "nourishment that does not nourish."

Just as it is impossible for meditators to reach deep meditation while the ego is present in their inner mental space, it is impossible for lovers to love in an unreserved way while the ego is present in their intimacy. Just as it is necessary for the meditator to lock the ego out of his inner space, it is necessary for the lovers to lock their egos out of their relationship.

When the one we love is dominated by his ego, as when he puts his love for us at the bottom of his hierarchy of interests, we have no choice but to lock his ego out of our inner space. This lockout must be permanent, meaning, we will never allow the ego-dominated self to return. This means we are adamant in not allowing our weak baby self to go along just to get along. It means we turn our backs (in our inner attitude) and go on our way, keeping disengaged from anything that the other's external ego-dominated self puts before us to notice.

This does not mean we are not polite, or that we are brusque, vindictive, unforgiving, or unkind. Nor does it mean we forget his imprisoned true self. (This is what various *I Ching* lines mean when they counsel us to "see the great man.") We continue to be true to our own natures: gentle, kind, and welcoming when the other's true self returns, but until then we remain adamantly firm in going on alone, minding our lives without regard to what his external ego-directed self does. In this way, we relate intrinsically, from our inner truth to the inner truth of the other. This enables us to preserve our dignity and self-esteem, and to send the correct inner messages.

Being adamant means we do not mind whether we ever see the other again, and we leave it entirely up to him whether or not he finds his way out of being oppressed by his ego. We only trust that following the good within ourselves will keep our life wholesome and good, and that we can be happy with the results, whatever they are. This is to trust the power of truth, the power of love, and the Cosmos.

In this way, we pay attention only to being true to ourselves. We pay no attention to the future or the past, nor do we lifeguard the other, through focusing on him with our inner eye. We live entirely in the present, content, wanting nothing, not looking outside ourselves for something.

If then one day our beloved presents himself to us in his true form, modestly and sincerely, we greet him with love. We go to meet him halfway, free of all anger and need for retribution. But in no way do we accept a partial reform, or any tests his ego may put forward, to see if it will be allowed back in. We are ever ready to do what inner duty requires: "ford the river with resolution," as it says in Hex. 11, Line 2, meaning, return to our solitary inner space.

Because the ego has such an enormous repertoire of tricks by which it can invade or dominate our personalities, it would be impossible to catalog them. The following, however, is a partial list of ways in which the ego presents problems to the love relationship that we need particularly to understand:

—its self-orientation, and vaingloriousness, in constantly seeking to be recognized, verified, pumped up, and otherwise supported.

—its requirement that all evidences of love be externally manifested.

—its readiness to quit with each disappointment.

—its lack of courage, through seeking to avoid the risk of love.

—its straight-line requirement that everything proceed straight and forthwith toward a recognizable, obvious goal. This often translates into the maxim, "The end justifies the means."

—its "want it now" orientation that leads to impatience, intolerance, and vindictiveness.

—its comparing attitude, by which it measures its progress in terms of envious comparisons, as for example, how others are succeeding while we are not.

—its compulsion to tie the love relationship down into ownership and security.

—its dependency on props. The beloved must keep bolstering our ego; it has a "feed me constantly" attitude.

—its feeling of rights, as in the attitude, "If the other loves me, then he ought to do this, and I have the right to do that."

—its denial of responsibility when it has been the cause of mistakes and injustices.

—its tendency to make vows and adopt rigid stances.

—its defensiveness when emotionally wounded, so that it immediately throws up barricades around the heart against any further risk and vulnerability; its anticipation of, and evasive action against, future wounds.

—its tendency to see things as fixed, bad times as permanently bad, and good times as lasting forever. When things go well, we are full of hope and exaggerated self-confidence; when things go badly, we are depressed, seeing no end to the misery.

—its promissory nature, attempting to bribe the loved one by doing or promising to do things that often cannot be performed; this accounts for its indulgence in flattery.

—its tendency toward reprisals in its efforts to vindicate itself and restore self-worth, even though such actions are counterproductive.

—its possessiveness, through enviously seeing the beloved's strengths and assets, and wanting to turn those talents to its benefit and to no one else's.

—its impostor nature, posing as the doer, the great lover, the problem solver, the great, glorious all-wise one, God.

—its energy-demanding nature; it depends entirely upon gaining recognition from others to exist, therefore it seeks constantly to put us in the view of others to gain recognition and feedback, even if it is only negative feedback. It is therefore invasive and encroaching.

It is essential that lovers avoid relating in ways that will encourage and enlarge each other's egos. This means they must follow certain rules within themselves. The most important of these rules is to retreat into reserve and caution when the other's ego is present, and to relate simply and openly when the other returns to being modest, simple, and open. In Hex. 55, the *I Ching* calls this, "going with the openings, retreating with the closings." By withdrawing into reserve and caution, one signals to the other, without saying anything, that an open, trusting relationship is endangered.

Hexagram 62, Line 5, likens withdrawal to being in a cave. In this line, it is the Sage that has withdrawn into the cave, presumably having retreated in the presence of our ego. We can draw it out again by returning to sincerity.

Withdrawal does not mean one abandons inner openness, or one's love for the other's true self; it means that one is firmly decided that the other's ego cannot be one's partner. One remains in withdrawal until it is safe to come out again, that is, when the other's true self, as is evidenced by modesty and sincerity, returns. In this way, the worth of one's personality is safeguarded and one's love is not thrown away on the other's ego. (See Hex. 41, Line 1).

While within one's cave, it is important to remember and hold to the other's true self. The *I Ching* likens this to being "one-eyed," as it is put in Hex. 54, Line 2. This refers to the *inner* sense of seeing that sees only the other's true self. In this way, one is able to remain loyal to that self, without connecting with, and energizing, the charade self. Through keeping one's love for the other intact, one supports and strengthens his true self. Relating in this way eventually enables the beloved to free himself from his fears, and thereby throw off the bondage of his ego.

Love alone has the power to dissolve the ego and to rescue another's true self to its rightful place as leader of the personality. Several lines of the *I Ching* speak directly of this rescue as the lover's duty, and loving the other as part of one's Cosmic assignments. (Hex. 13, Line 5, and Hex. 39. Line 6.) The rescue is achieved through loving the other's true self, thereby enabling it to reopen his closed heart so that he can live fully and be able to receive and give love in a complete reciprocity. It means that one's trust in the life process as a positive creative force, is revived; likewise, one's life force, or *chi* energy and will to live, are revived.

Love, like kindness, arises from inner necessity. It is a complete and spontaneous expression of one's nature. To deny love is to deny one's existence. To deny the great love of one's life is to nullify a part, if not all, of one's vital force. It is to block that which is completely healing, both to the self, and to the beloved. The ego is an enemy to this freeing process. Through limiting the experience of love, it reduces life to a narrow rigidity that constricts the life force and extinguishes it through hopelessness.

In the love relationship, it is necessary to be constantly vigilant against the ego. Especially after periods when things go well, one tends to think that the ego is no longer a threat. Precisely then its first whisperings begin, "You don't need to worry, you have it made." Reaching for dominance, it begins to encroach on the other presumptuously. It is necessary, always and forever, to be on guard against such subtle attempts to shut down loving, and to regain protective distance from the other under the pretense of protecting oneself. Bad moods mean that this is happening. Keeping open is the daily work of loving. The lovers will fail, time and again, because ego habits are strong, but by persisting in these efforts, by returning conscientiously to serving the love they have for each other, by nourishing each other with good thoughts, as it is counselled in Hex. 37, Line 4, and by continuing to forgive each other for their lapses, they will break these habits, and in the process learn how to make love stay.

Love, therefore, requires attention, awareness, and the willingness to keep disciplined. It requires that we learn to recognize, and keep free of our egos, for as it is said in Hex. 60, Line 5, we cannot limit others successfully if we have not first limited ourselves.

Lovers need constantly to forgive themselves, because learning to love is a process that requires making mistakes and blundering. Sometimes it is only through painful experiences that we learn not to hurt, and to be careful and conscientious. Misunderstanding is often necessary before people can fully understand. A great deal of growth is required before we successfully learn not to want. But only through such a process is it possible to awaken and develop the true self, which is necessary if the love is to find its fulfillment and completion. It is paradoxical that we cannot seek the completion of love as a goal, just as we cannot seek joy as a goal. Because they are gifts of the Cosmos, they are the consequences of being in harmony with oneself. The most direct path, therefore, goes in a seemingly opposite direction to seeking love as a goal, namely, by being loyal first and foremost to one's true self and one's inner dignity.

The ego's reach for dominance is based on the view that, "Someone must be in charge of the ship." In the love relationship, however, there is not one ship, but two. The two can go in convoy, but not in one ship with one captain. No one can rightly take over for another his responsibility to the Cosmos, or his responsibility to his conscience and inner sense of truth. The two ships can travel together, cooperating, sharing, and loving, but each partner must still be master of himself.

Chapter 8

Inner Communications and the Nourishing Love Response

Once the love contact between two people occurs, it is naturally accompanied by the lovers' spontaneous thoughts of each other. These thoughts, which in the first bloom of love preoccupy the mind and linger pleasantly, travel back and forth through the lovers' inner channel of communication. They feel bound to the other in some mysterious way, and although physically they may be thousands of miles apart, they reside happily with each other. The magnetism and intensity of these thoughts demonstrate the power of the inner unity that has been established between them.

This inner communication is often accompanied by the feeling that they are actually in the other's physical presence, in an embrace which holds them fast together. This inner-felt embrace is their best proof that an inner connection has been established between them and is the lovers' inner reality. Feelings of connectedness are constantly present. They may be felt by one, or both at the same time. When they feel them simultaneously, these feelings greatly intensify. When one of them no longer feels the other's presence, it does not mean that their unity has ceased to exist, but that he has become separated from accessing his inner feelings. The cause of this separation, invariably, is the presence of the ego, with its fears, doubts, and resistances.

Certain inner connections and channels of communication exist between all of us. We receive messages through these inner channels in the form of what people describe as vibrations or emanations. The strength of inner connections varies. Every day we receive emanations from people. The child, who is more strongly attuned to his inner feelings than acculturated adults, immediately perceives whether the adults around him are friendly or not. Children who have not been filled with distrust will be drawn toward people who are open to them. They will remain reticent, turn away, or even react irrationally in the presence of people who are closed. People are unconsciously aware of each other's positive and negative vibrations. They are consciously aware, as well, if they have strong psychic abilities.

Many of the problems we encounter in daily life are generated by fears, doubts, and hesitations, to which people react. Thus, inasmuch as we doubt and fear, we create our reality, often generating the very thing we fear. Because we have this capacity to create good or evil, the *I Ching* constantly counsels us to pay attention to the thoughts and feelings we allow to inhabit our minds and hearts. Pure and good thoughts always have good effects (Hex. 31, Line 4). Trivial, picayune, and negative thoughts have bad effects (Hex. 56, Line 1). Allowing these is what Hex. 44, Line 1, calls "feeding the pig," and what Hex. 48, Line 1, calls "drinking the mud of the well." Hex. 27, Line 3, regards such thoughts as "nourishment that does not nourish." We are counseled, therefore, not to allow ourselves to indulge in luxurious, immodest, ego-centered thoughts. If we retain an inner awareness, we will be able to retreat from such thoughts the instant they appear (Hex. 16, Line 2).

In the love relationship, this ability to communicate on the inner level is much stronger than everyday inner communications between people. The *I Ching* describes this ability in Hex. 61, Line 2:

> "A crane calling in the shade.
> Its young answers it.
> I have a good goblet.
> I will share it with you."

Wilhelm comments that this phrase "refers to the involuntary influence of a man's inner being upon persons of kindred spirit. The crane need not show itself on a high hill. It may be quite hidden when it sounds its call; yet its young will hear its note, will recognize it and give answer. Where there is a joyous mood, there a comrade will appear to share a glass of wine.

"This is the echo awakened in men through spiritual attraction. Whenever a feeling is voiced with truth and frankness, whenever a deed is the clear expression of sentiment, a mysterious and far-reaching influence is exerted. At first it acts on those who are inwardly receptive. But the circle grows larger and larger. The root of all influence lies in one's own inner being: given true and vigorous expression in word and deed, its effect is great. The effect is but the reflection of something that emanates from one's own heart. Any deliberate intention of an effect would only destroy the possibility of producing it."

In the love situation, all loving thoughts and feelings are healthy and good. They communicate through the inner channel as the essential nourishment of love. These feelings happen automatically and without any conscious design. They are powerful in the first stages of love, sweeping through the lovers without encountering any form of resistance. Later, however, after the first misunderstanding, they occur more as back-of-the-mind thoughts and repressed feelings, because, in fact, they have been declared invalid by the ego.

It is particularly important, during the difficult times at the beginning when misunderstandings separate the lovers, that they keep the inner channel open, so that their loving contact with each other remains unobstructed. This is not done by consciously wanting to renew contact with the beloved, but by making a conscious effort to resist the encroaching fears and doubts, thus keep them from taking root in one's mind and heart. One resists all forms of hopelessness and avoids focusing on the external charades of the other's ego; one clings to the validity of what one originally felt about the other. Because trust in these feelings will be tested, the lover needs to access the help that is available in the nourishing love response. Needless to say, it is particularly helpful in such times of crisis to consult the *I Ching*.

The nourishing love response occurs when we consciously and actively respond to feelings, however faint, which come from the beloved through the inner channel. The power of this response lies in the fact that it is a conscious affirmation of feelings that come from the unconscious. The more fully and freely we are able to make this conscious response, the more [illegible] ecomes.

[illegible] hing love response occurs on the outer plane [illegible] external expressions of love, from affectionate embraces to the full sexual expression of love. On this level, the effects are immediately seen and felt. We do not, however, ordinarily recognize the nourishing quality of love which occurs in the smallest and most hidden expressions of affection and passion. For example, we do not recognize that anything of importance is happening when we write a heartfelt love letter, nevertheless, such an action has a powerful, nourishing effect, whether it is sent or not. The nourishing love response occurs whenever words and actions actively express our inner feelings.

Just as the expressions of love that are seen are a natural part of loving, so do all expressions of love that are not seen. To the ego, they seem silly and humiliating because they lack glory, are too unpretentious, too blatant, too simpleminded, and too sincere.

Many a lover has treasured, nearly with his life, jewelry or other valued objects that he has associated with his beloved. Humorous playwrights and novelists poke fun at lovers hugging pillows and kissing photographs, but these too are responses to emanations that come through the inner channel from the other. They are legitimate because they reciprocate the other's feelings in a fully conscious, active way. These actions complete the circuit of energy that nourishes and supports both through the inner channel. When lovers are far away from each other or isolated through misunderstanding, such acts maintain their love, keeping it warm and alive. When they ignore and repress these impulses because they seem ridiculous and are such a humble way of expressing love, "the heart suffocates," as stated in Hex. 52, Line 3.

When the conscious mind is in harmony with the unconscious inner self, the lover is automatically in contact with the inner psyche of the beloved, joined with him in the bond of love, and placed in the nourishing flow of loving energy. When the conscious mind is out of harmony with the inner self, the lover loses this feeling of connectedness and the sense of well-being that accompanies it. The more they become out of harmony with themselves, the more desolate they feel.

When both come into harmony with themselves at the same time, both consciously and intensely feel themselves to be in the other's presence; when both give conscious affirmation to their feelings at the same time, the power of these feelings multiplies. People in love often corroborate with each other the precise times when they have felt the other's presence so strongly. Many lovers experience times when they have been awakened during the middle of the night by the other's conscious affirmation of his feelings of love, even though they were far apart from each other.

The spontaneous welling up of these feelings into consciousness presents the lovers with an opportunity to consciously accept and embrace them. Making this conscious choice is similar to the Cosmic opportunity we are given to "see" another's true self. Nearly all of us can recall at least one person in our lives who did nothing more than see that self in us, and for precisely this reason has been of crucial importance in our lives. So it is with the nourishing love response. It is a conscious decision to go with our innermost feelings. It not only affirms the true self of the beloved, it affirms who we are and what life is about, because it is a choice for feeling and living over thinking without feeling, and denying living. From this humble and modest beginning agreement between one's conscious mind and the humble feelings of the heart, true love grows and mounts in strength.

From a Cosmic point of view, it is harmonious and correct to make this choice. Likewise, it is disharmonious and incorrect to deny, reject, or push away even the smallest of such feelings, for to do so denies both oneself and the beloved the vital *chi* nourishment needed to strengthen and free their true selves. The nourishing love response works both ways simultaneously. It keeps the lovers warmly attached on the inner level while they find their way past the fears and doubts which obstruct the outward expression of their love.

Through the conscious affirmation of one's love, one makes the other central to one's life. In a sense it is an act of abandonment, not of self, but of the fear that holds one back from being oneself. The act of conscious affirmation is like jumping a horse over a fence, or taking one's feet off the bottom to swim. In doing it, we find that we cross over into a new territory. There we are freed to love in the broader, all-inclusive way that sees only the other's true self and never believes in his ego charade.

To the ego, of course, receiving and expressing love so modestly is the ultimate humiliation, since it excludes the approval and verification it wants from the love relationship. Nevertheless, this humiliation of the ego is necessary before one can develop the true humility needed for love to be able to manifest itself externally. Nourished and protected in the dark womb of the innermost self, the lovers' inner bond grows ever larger and stronger until the ego can no longer threaten it.

Every time we allow the ego to interfere, we cut ourselves off from the all-important nourishment. This loss is always painful. But going away from oneself in this manner is like stretching a rubber band to its limit; when we are hurt enough, we return to ourselves in real humility. Return renews the inner bond. When the inner bond can no longer be invaded and interrupted by the ego, external obstructions dissolve. Then inner content manifests externally. As it is put in Hex. 22, Line 6, "Form no longer conceals content, but brings out its value to the full."

Each of the two love partners must do his inner work

separately, without regard to what the other does or does not do. He must do it without looking aside to see if the other is doing his share. When one looks aside, as Hex. 61, Line 4, puts it, "the team horse goes astray." It is important that neither lover allows his ego to compare what he does with what his "team mate" does, otherwise he will lose his will to see the work through to completion.

In nature, every birth has its beginnings in a similar hidden way. In the womb or the egg, for example, the tiny cells are kept warm and protected until the form becomes complete. Then the organism can emerge into the world. The free-willed love relationship must also develop organically.

Since the nourishing love response can only be consciously received when one is in harmony with his innermost self, maintaining inner harmony is the main work of love. This means that one does not allow the ego to introject doubt, either about the correctness of the relationship, or about its having the blessings of the Cosmos. It is necessary to acknowledge, without reservation, that one is meant to follow this love wholeheartedly.

To follow one's love with all one's heart is what in Hex. 27, Line 1, is called the "magic tortoise." The commentary says, "The magic tortoise is a creature possessed of such supernatural powers that it lives on air and needs no earthly nourishment." The magic tortoise is the enlivened and buoyant support one receives from the nourishing love response. We lose the magic tortoise when we doubt the inner connection, when we are too proud to respond in the humble way indicated, or when we avoid responding when the other is open to us.

During times when the lovers are separated by misunderstanding, Hex. 38, Line 2, says, "He meets his lord in a narrow street." The commentary explains that although it has become impossible for the lovers to meet each other in the usual way, because of misunderstandings that have arisen, there is nevertheless a "narrow street" where they may meet. This is a metaphor for the nourishing love response which enables them to remain united. As the commentary of Hex. 13, Line 5, says, "Two people are outwardly separated, but in their hearts they are united. They are kept apart by their positions in life. Many difficulties and obstructions arise between them and cause them grief. But, remaining true to each other, they allow nothing to separate them, and although it costs them a severe struggle to overcome the obstacles, they will succeed. When they come together their sadness will change to joy."

Because the difficulties at the beginning are greatly increased if the lovers become sexually intimate before the foundation for their relationship has been established, it is meant that their relationship develop only on the inner level at first. Their experience of each other's presence on this invisible level teaches them about the power of their love, its ability to sustain them, and that they can trust their inner feelings about each other. Their trust in each other becomes so strong that distrust no longer enters. Their ability to sense each other's feelings becomes so well developed that each knows exactly what the other thinks and feels, so that they no longer mistake or misunderstand each other through what is said. Such a strong inner bond cannot be created in any other way.

We need to be aware that bad feelings are also a form of nourishment. For example, when we consciously cling to ill feelings toward the other, the *I Ching*, in Hex. 21, Line 3, refers to this as punishment by the ego. Although such punishment seems to be justified, it creates what the I Ching regards as wars and lawsuits, which may last for years. There is no Cosmic justification for our ego to punish another. Such punishment invariably rebounds upon us as feelings of isolation, misery, and self-conflict.

When a lover no longer can feel the other's inner presence, it is time for him to look within at the thoughts he is allowing in his mind. Hex. 47, Line 3, pictures a situation in which "a man permits himself to be oppressed by stone, and leans on thorns and thistles. He enters his house and does not see his wife. Misfortune." This refers, the commentary adds, "to his leaning on things that have in themselves no stability and that are merely a hazard for him who leans on them. Thereupon he turns back irresolutely and retires into his house, only to find, as a fresh disappointment, that his wife is not there." Leaning on doubts and becoming focused on the other's negative characteristics, causes the beloved to disappear from the mind's eye. His image becomes indistinct, like a photograph that has become faded by light. Also, the lover's presence can no longer be felt. To reestablish access to the inner connection, it is necessary to regain a true perspective and to see the beloved as whole and perfect. Hex. 38, Line 6, notes that the disappearance of the beloved from one's inner view happens because we fail to see him as he really is. We have become "isolated through opposition. One sees one's companion as a pig covered with dirt...as unclean as a dirty pig and as dangerous as a wagon full of devils." Then one "adopts an attitude of defense. But in the end, realizing his mistake, he perceives that the other is approaching with the best intentions for the purpose of close union." Once we become aware that our ego has been thrusting these images before our inner eye, we are able to repossess again our inner space. By consciously rejecting the ego and its suggestions, the inner connection becomes reestablished and it is once more possible to feel, as Confucius said, "my heart in sympathy with yours," and to see the other's true self.

One cannot consciously try to reestablish access to the other through the inner channel by trying to love him. Access can be reestablished only by correcting one's conscious view of the other. Nor can one nourish the other through conscious attempts to project thoughts to him. Such ego-directed effort conveys only the doubts that make one strive in this way. All striving is ego driven. When love comes from humility, it is in harmony with the whole Cosmos and therefore can flow freely from its Cosmic source to its destination.

Desire blocks one's access to the inner channel. Lovers naturally long to be with each other, but desire is a fear-driven pressure to end doubt-inspired feelings of ambiguity. Doubt arises when the ego focuses on wanting to be recognized and affirmed. This effort is invariably perceived by the beloved and resisted. Desire arises from the need to ameliorate the negative feelings that accompany doubt. We do not desire what we already have, or know with certainty is ours. Desire hangs upon the attainment of an imagined relief that will be felt when the love is proven. But love cannot be proven in this way. Love gained through desire is never believed, and for this reason it does not satisfy. All attempts by the ego to attain love through force only end in throwing oneself away, which brings still another set of negative dynamics.

When a lover doubts his inner knowledge about the beloved, he suffers self-conflict; his ego may then demand either that he forget the relationship, or abandon his principles to do whatever it takes to make the situation work. The more he acts on these doubts, the greater and more painful his self-conflict becomes. The problem can only be solved through refusing to listen to doubt, and to give up trying to answer the myriad questions of self-conflict. Leaving the doubts unanswered is what the *I Ching* calls withdrawing from conflict at the beginning. Questions aroused by self-conflict cannot be answered, for each answer only opens up another doubt, which in turn generates yet another question. Withdrawal from trying to answer questions of doubt enables a person to become free from domination by his ego, and to return to inner calm.

The nourishing love response depends upon a lover's discipline to keep the inner channel between them open. He does this through keeping his thoughts of the beloved wholly good, and by regarding the challenges of the relationship positively, as perfect for the growth and needs of the true self. He maintains his openness to respond, keeps his heart free of barricades, and allows no wedges of doubt to separate them. He feels, and is then strengthened by, the love that flows reciprocally between their inner selves. Following this path leads to the externalizing of their love in an enduring way.

Fantasy

It is important to distinguish inner feelings from fantasy. Fantasy is a parade of images that glorify the ego. For example, our partner is seen as appreciating our wit, intelligence, good looks, or heroic accomplishments. Such fantasies show oneself as being verified, coddled, and attended to. The beloved is seen as important because he flatters our vanity, or adds to our wealth and power. We become obsessed with the beloved's good looks, outgoing personality, social position, or sophistication, because it impresses others.

Such ego-led fantasies harm the true love relationship. They project scenarios of what one thinks should happen. Although imagining the future has the positive aspect of helping lovers work out the practical details of their lives, when this imagining sets up expectations as to how things should happen, disappointments and misunderstandings follow. Love cannot follow a pre-written script. If a lover has fantasized about what is to happen on a certain date, he may then begin to expect things to happen, placing a negative pressure on the other. Fantasies that create expectations lead to disappointment and distrust.

Fantasies about the future have the effect of removing us from what is actually happening in the moment. It is as if we fantasize how a tennis ball is going to be served. When the serve then comes across the net differently, as it is bound to do, we are so engrossed in our planned response that we are unable to react as needed.

Fantasies about the future make us see only what we want to see, so that we gloss over inequities or insensitivities that occur. Such fantasies rob us of the awareness we need in order to respond creatively to the ongoing dynamics of the relationship.

Fantasizing about the future destroys the spontaneity of love. If the lover dreams, for example, how the next steps of their relating will occur, as in making love, their spontaneity becomes inhibited in favor of a contrived approach. Thus, instead of experiencing innocent tenderness and feeling, they experience awkwardness and embarrassment. Equally problematical and harmful is fantasizing to stimulate sexual feelings. This is "nourishment that does not nourish," as it is put in Hex. 27, Line 3.

The most dangerous aspect of fantasy happens when the lovers prefer an inner fantasy relationship to the experience of real love. The ego supports this, hoping to escape its own dissolution. Because the ego always pretends that it serves our safety and protection, it would make our lives a pre-written script. This, no doubt, is the appeal provided by romance novels, operas, TV soaps, X-rated movies, or even pornography, which present to the viewer a proxy life of imagined love and sensation. Many ego-dominated people seek security at all costs, therefore will substitute life, love, and intimacy by such proxies.

The inner relating that goes on naturally between two lovers at the beginning of their relationship is also a sort of proxy relationship, in that it must progress largely on the inner level of consciousness. But this period is meant to serve only as a preparatory stage that leads to their external unification. Especially when there are strong mental objections to the beloved, as to his religion, family, class, etc., the relationship might become stranded, unable to progress out of the proxy stage.

The fact remains that people do not have control over whom they fall in love with. One may fall in love with another who is regarded as unacceptable. One will, therefore, deny the other's importance to oneself on the external level, yet try to keep him in one's life in a proxy way. This keeps the relationship in a sort of "no man's land," so that the one denying the relationship oppresses the other. Dr. Rank, in Ibsen's play, *A Doll's House* , is an example of such a relationship.

A proxy relationship can continue in this way only as long as the one oppressed accepts this treatment. He can correct this problem by firmly making up his mind that the unjust situation is unacceptable and wrong. If he excuses the situation as "the best that can be done," nothing will be done. The *I Ching* calls this sort of weakness a "luxurious attitude" in Hex. 63, Line 5, and a "comfortable approach" in Hex. 19, Line 3. Only when the oppressed becomes firm can the oppressor perceive the necessity to relate correctly.

In the meantime, it is important that while saying a resolute inner No to the oppressing treatment, the oppressed not blame the oppressor. Nor should he, through impatience, doubt, or a desire for justice, indulge in vindictiveness and alienation, but give time and space for the oppressor to correct himself. One needs to realize that the oppressor may be holding back because of deep inner fears based on social custom or religion. After saying the inner No and retreating inwardly into neutrality, the *I Ching* recommends turning the matter over to the Cosmos for rectification.

Chapter 9

The Essentials of Relating

When two people meet one another halfway, it is, as the *I Ching* puts it, a time of great unification. The expression in the *I Ching*, "coming to meet halfway," (Hex. 44) means just that: two people come to meet each other halfway. This defines the free-willed relationship that is based on natural inclination, without any "musts" or "must-not's" attached.

Meeting halfway means that each keeps conscious of and observes certain basic principles of relating, of his own free will. Each does this through a conscientiousness that he has begun to understand is necessary to their unity. Each does this from an understanding that these principles are necessary to enable their unity. Each does this because, through the difficulties that they have encountered in the beginning, they have recognized and accepted their mutual destiny and relatedness, and their natural dependence, each upon the other, and upon the Cosmos as the source of their love.

They have recognized, additionally, that their responsibility to the other is synonymous with their responsibility to the

Cosmos, which has presented them with the other to love. As the *I Ching* puts it in Hex. 19, "Their approach towards each other has come from a high place." The completion of their meeting happens when both have made the great and necessary effort required to displace, within themselves, the dominance of their egos. This completion manifests itself, at last, in their joyful and enduring unity. Only such a powerful force as love can drive lovers to do the work required, while giving that work all the joy and sorrow, the happiness and longing, the bliss and suffering, enabling them to experience life at its fullest.

The principles of relating that they learn during the difficult period at the beginning become a complete operating system of attitudes that forms a perfect foundation for their love to grow and bloom. It does so in such a way that their love overflows to everyone around them, creating a still greater unity in their lives with others. These principles of relating are as vitamins are to the body, essential to the health and duration of their love and mutual happiness. The absence of any one can wound, cripple, or destroy their harmony, and if it persists, their relationship as well.

There are fundamental limits that are natural to relationships. If we know these limits, we will be able to avoid damaging the supports upon which the love relationship is ever dependent.

Although we are taught by our culture to think that life is what we think it is about, and what we think we are, life is really about what we feel we are. In the deepest center of self, we do not think, we feel. To feel is to live; to think without feeling is to put life on hold.

In a meditation, loving another was presented in a single image as waking up suddenly to find that the two lovers were attached to each other by the breastbone, as in Siamese twins.

Something in me immediately rebelled in horror and it was not clear then what this meant. Over time I came to see that it was synonymous with the common image given by society that the love relationship is a unity into which both merge themselves by becoming one. It was clear, however, that as Siamese twins, both were extremely hampered in their movements and tied to each other in an obviously cruel and unnatural way. Not long afterwards I was walking with a friend on a beach who described a sort of training she did with people to help them define their limits. She drew a large figure-eight in the sand and told me to stand in one of the circles. "Now occupy the circle completely! Walk all over it and then jump up and down, shouting, "This space is mine!" After I had done this she then said that the other space represented the intrinsic space everyone else has. She said that whether that person is your mother, your lover, your friend, or your foe, you enter their space only by their invitation, and you allow them to enter yours only by your invitation. The place where the two circles meet is love. I have since realized with gratitude the validity of this experience, and how until we have "claimed" our intrinsic (inner) space, others walk into it as if they have a right, tell us what to do, what is wrong with us, and the like. When we claim and own our inner space, up to the very last inch of it, others respect our space. We also respect their spaces when we do not tell them what is wrong with them, and what they "ought" to do and think. We respond to them by saying what feels correct for us to do, to engage in, to think, or to accept. It is this respect for our inner space and theirs that constitutes our dignity and self-esteem.

Keeping this kind of connection with the beloved, interdependency does not degenerate into dependency, and love does not fall into emotional attachment. The kind of bond where both form one unity, as in the Siamese twin model, results in a suffocation of the relationship, and an extreme need, eventually, to end it, or if not end it, to cheat on it.

This kind of bond is not to be confused with the inner connection between two lovers, and the kind of thrashing about of the ego as it refuses the relationship unless it can control it. When the two begin to accept the inner unity that exists between them, they become exhilarated to find that the other suits them in all respects, and that it is wonderful to be close and loving, receiving and radiating the nourishment that fulfills their deepest inner needs.

The disparity between these two contrary feelings, the resistance and flailing about of the ego, as it resists any form of relatedness as a loss of independence, and the delight of the true self with the other, creates the conflict that is necessary to bring to the surface the destructive attitudes that one or the other has been holding. This surfacing gives the inner self an opportunity to cast off the ego bonds that have enslaved it. The work of discovering and dredging up from the depths, root fears, misconceptions, and doubts about life that have caused the true self to relinquish control, is necessarily gradual. Hex. 48, Line 4, refers to this period as "lining the well, so that the water stays clear." Gradually, each begins to accept their relatedness and love it, finding great joy in embracing the other inwardly.

The process by which all this is brought about creates a wider, broader outlook. This more complete outlook is like installing into one's computer a new program that is capable of doing much more work than the old one. To do this work, however, often requires that one upgrade the computer to a greater capacity, meaning, a bigger heart, a larger degree of patience, and a more intense dedication to the task of distinguishing what is truly important from what is vain, egocentric, and only leading to suffering. The newer program is based on values that are completely in harmony with the Cosmic Order.

In a meditation, the human mind was presented as being somewhat like a computer. This can be seen as logically true, as well, simply because of the way the human mind has simulated itself in the creation of the computer. The computer, like the mind, interfaces with its memory. When a program is first installed, the computer creates a route to the memory so that it can access the program and do the work. Then it memorizes the route. Sometimes, when a large number of programs to do different things are loaded, the routing becomes tangled. It is desirable at intervals, therefore, to "rebuild the desktop," or to "reformat the driver," as it is variously called. This enables the routes to be recreated in an orderly fashion, and the programs to work smoothly.

Similar things happen in the mind. Through force of habit and long-established ways of routing and evaluating information and experience, we make new insights and improved ways of relating virtually impossible. Old fears and doubts are activated automatically upon encountering experiences that we have always designated as negative. Immediately, the experience is dumped into a compartment reserved for bad feelings that are then excited and replayed, before we have had a chance to evaluate the experience in terms of our newer, better program. The newer program, for instance, might have seen the event as completely necessary for a further correction of the relationship to be made, so that patience, rather than impatience, would be one's automatic response. To move past fundamentally inadequate programs, it is necessary to "rebuild our desktop."

Such negative reactions may continue to happen even though we have already trained ourselves to react differently. In such cases, we find ourselves at a loss to see why we continue to fall back into the old patterns. The image of the desktop is valuable here, because it hints that it is necessary to take out all the old memories that produce negative emotions and really look at them. We put them on the table in order to see all their positive aspects. A meditation image suggested that such memories are like tarnished silver objects. On first glance, they seem to be worthless, but after polishing, are both beautiful and valuable, worth storing in the Fort Knox area of one's mind.

Development of the true self requires that we understand and re-file our experiences in the most positive ways possible. We clean out the cesspool of the mind into which we have routed negative ideas, and blow away all the ill feelings that have been attached to each experience. Then we will see only good and positive things, and our "army," as the *I Ching* calls the disciplined self, will be in perfect order, strong, and able to stand up to the challenges of the ego. When this strength is sufficient, all obstructions to the lovers' unity will have been removed.

A number of positive attitudes are essential to loving, although it is true that love can exist for a time without any of these being consciously practiced by either one of the lovers. At first, for example, they will have a natural hesitation that is neither trust nor distrust. For their love to be free to fully manifest itself, hesitation must give way to trust. This is possible only by their building confidence in each other's willingness to deal with the ego.

Because of common attitudes present in our culture, most people approach relationships with a certain amount of distrust. For example, a man may hold the common male view that women come with "baggage" that he, as a man, will be expected to carry. He will tend, therefore, to inspect each prospective woman in terms of this baggage, to see what will be expected of him. During the first days or hours of love, when he has met the one with whom he is truly mated on the inner level, such thoughts will have been temporarily suspended, simply through the shock of love. But soon the old negative idea of baggage will reemerge. If their love is to survive beyond this bare beginning, he must enlarge his mental program to realize that whatever her baggage, it is not for him to bear, but rather to help her strengthen her true self to free herself of it.

Trust

Trust and love are nearly synonymous, for when the instant trust is removed from a relationship, feelings of attraction and love cool. Outright distrust turns these feelings quickly to ice. Trust, therefore, is essential to love and is the condition that makes the lovers' interdependence and cooperation possible. Without trust, interdependency is full of pain and error.

Trust is an attitude Coleridge described as a "willing suspension of disbelief." It is not dismissing or overlooking the other's transgressions and errors, but acknowledging them and saying an inner No to them, and then turning them over to the Cosmos for resolution. The inner No transmits to him through the inner channel, while the suspension of disbelief gives him time to reflect, and the absence of censure that allows his true self time to respond without a loss of face. It further keeps one's own mind open in the recognition that mistakes and transgressions are necessary to bring the ego, with its false ideas, into the open, so that the correct limits may be set. Responding in this way is in accord with the harmonious workings of the Cosmos, and draws its help to restore harmony. This kind of giving space is not to be confused with compassion, which would be an inner sanctioning of the other's bad treatment. The inner No is like the fence around one's property: it is there to keep out all destructive ego behavior. Failing to say the inner No equals giving permission to the other to transgress.

Meanwhile, it is necessary to make sure that one's own attitudes are not part of the problem, as when we act with impatience. People frequently hold back their innermost feelings because they sense that we would swiftly transfer onto them childish attachments, or that we hold conventional ideas of relationship that would require them to sacrifice their inner truth or their inner freedom. They unconsciously sense in whatever way our ego would trap them and destroy their true feelings.

Indeed, the love relationship shows us that if either partner is distancing himself from the other, the ego of one or the other is present. Both are led, if they will persevere long enough to see what the love relationship wants to teach them, to discover the deceptions and interferences that their egos present. They see how the ego's guidance, time and again, has led only to their suffering and humiliation. Once each has "deleted" a substantial amount of the old program, thus unblocking his natural program with its larger views, they begin to trust events that otherwise would greatly disturb them. As they recognize the reliability of these greater perspectives, their trust in the way they feel becomes installed as a fully working system. Their experiences correspond to what the *I Ching* calls "inner truth." Holding to their inner truth keeps them from being undermined by the doubts that accompany the purely mental conjecture and hoping engaged in by the ego.

While this awareness is being developed, their trust needs to be in the nature of a willing suspension of disbelief that enables each to extend patience and loyalty while the other goes through the necessary experiences to learn. Both are certain, in the course of events, to make mistakes, and to fail each other in some way. The one disappointed must not be put off by this, but hold to his inner bond. If, instead, he continues to focus on the external situation, assigning to it all the old reasons and blame, his distrust will soon turn into a dangerous alienation that will wreak havoc on their relationship. If he will remember to cling to and trust the inner reality that he has felt, and to his knowledge of the other's great and good self, he will be able to correct the situation simply by what he communicates through their inner connection.

This practice must be carried out in the presence of the impatient ego, which always seeks to undermine one's will to carry one's task to its completion. (See the Judgment in Hex. 15.) The ego will put forth, for quite some time, reasons to distrust, to not wait, to point out that self-interest is not being served. These attacks by the ego, and one's conscious rejection of them, is the work lovers must do on themselves. With every misunderstanding, with every transgression, the ego will use the opportunity to put pressure on their love to cool; the lover must always keep his love warm. The ego will put pressure on him to build protective barricades around his heart; he must recognize and dismantle these efforts. His ego will wish to attain power and influence by placing importance on being the chief one in the beloved's heart (even though his true self is, already); it will demand more than is given, for enough is never enough to the ego. This careful, constant conscientiousness is what the *I Ching* means by modesty.

Trust means to trust this process which goes two steps forward and one backward. The lovers need to trust the bond between them and the power of their love to find its own way of emerging, in its own time. They need to trust the validity and reality of the assignment they have been given by the Cosmos to rescue each other's true selves, through believing in them.

Trust means that the lovers trust that a full and free sexual expression of their love completes their inner feelings for each other. Tradition and degraded views of sexuality have greatly harmed our free and innocent ability to express love sexually. A new sort of trust must be developed, and this requires that both lovers work through the decadent ideas regarding male and female sexuality that derive from patriarchal-based religions. These attitudes not only deny sexuality to be an essential expression of love, they desensitize and even brutalize the love relationship. These traditions have cast males into a false bravado of dominance that keeps men forever pampered and spoiled in their view of themselves, unable to mature. Females, on the other hand, are presented with the choice of accepting either the sterile image of the sexually unblemished Virgin Mary, or else accept their sexuality as impure and unworthy. With this degraded view of their natures, they easily accept the idea of male superiority and domination.

Even modern psychiatry is partly infected with such religious-based ideas that females are merely defective males born without a penis. This idea gave rise to what Freud called "penis envy." According to this patriarchal thinking, the "correct" sexual position for a woman is underneath the man, yielding to his dominance, and any other position is considered to be an aberration. Such false, superimposed models, stemming from the Biblical notion that *man* was created to dominate the earth, and everything on it, give rise to sexual aggression and abuse.

Attitudes derived from this tradition are responsible for the fact that in the United States one out of every six married women is reported to have been raped by her husband. These same attitudes are also the basis for the success of movies based on the hero being a macho man who subdues and dominates the strong and independent woman; and they are responsible for the high acceptance of violence that is shown daily on television. Many published studies have noted the damage that such attitudes do to children who grow up with these defective parental role models.

Once the psyche has been freed from such decadent ideas, the lovers will not need to attempt to use the device of false sexuality as a substitute for feeling close to each other. Instead, when natural feelings of attraction and sexuality are absent, they will look within themselves to find the distrust that blocks their inner channel to each other. In this way, they will restore the integrity of their love, which at its root is trust. This will reawaken attraction and the sexual feelings that naturally accompany it.

Loyalty

The *I Ching* makes it clear, throughout its text, that a person's first and foremost loyalty must be to his inner truth, for it is from this inner truth that his loyalty to another's true self is made possible. The inner connection is in itself a kind of loyalty that is formed by the attraction that exists between the two lovers true selves. It is not something that can be contrived, as in something we "should" have towards our partner. For indeed, we cannot, nor should we be loyal to the other's ego. It is precisely this kind of abstract and all-inclusive loyalty that gives permission to the ego of one's beloved to be dominant, to act out, and to ultimately do all those things that damage and ruin the relationship. We see this damage occur in marriages where one of the partners is alcoholic, and the other enables his habit through covering up for the partner when he has broken the law or beat the children.

During such times when the true self of another is eclipsed by his ego, the loyalty one can have is to recognize that the other's true self is being embarrassed by its allowing the ego to do things that are against his own dignity. In all such situations, the first loyalty is to one's inner truth and self-respect, which means not to tolerate evil behavior, either through an inner denial that pushes it under the rug, or by sacrificing common sense and self-respect through a selfless and passive enduring, or a devotion to the self-image of "being a loyal person." A person who is loyal to a "good" self-image does so because he finds comfort in thinking he is superior to others—yet another aspect of the ego. It has nothing to do with being loyal to one's inner truth and common sense.

A person's inner truth, being his innermost feeling of love for the other's true self, and for their essential complementarity, acts as a loyalty to the other's true self, and to their connectedness. It is *not* loyalty to either's ego in any of the forms in which it shows itself, as a self-image, or as race, class, or position in society. It is this latter kind of loyalty that betrays both of their true selves. All of the issues of loyalty in a relationship need to circle around the one issue of the loyalty each has to his deepest inner truth.

Such a loyalty is betrayed whenever one of the partners listens to complaints, suspicions, or gossip about the other that would make him doubt his inner truth. The correct response to such situations is an inner No, "No, I will not participate in this!" Loyalty is also betrayed when the partner allows himself to assemble negative "files" in his mind about the other, when his inner feelings tell him otherwise. The reverse can also be true, that he may feel something is wrong in the relationship without there being any outward evidence. It is important that he pay attention to these inner warnings, for it means that negative thoughts may be active in the other's mind.

Loyalty is a natural part of the inner connection with the other. Upon seeing the other's true self with the inner eye, that image is imprinted in the memory of the heart. It causes the lovers to extend patience when there seems to be no basis for patience, and one to wait while the other works through his own inner problems. When one is true to this inner imprint, or vision of the other's potential, he strengthens the other's true self and helps him free himself from his ego. But it is also loyalty to one's inner truth that causes one to correctly withdraw when the other's ego is present. It is likewise loyalty to even leave the beloved behind and go on with one's life, if the other continues obstinately in his ego patterns beyond a reasonable and fair time. Love, as a Cosmic gift, is given to two people as an *opportunity* to realize themselves. If a person's ego is too entrenched to allow the opportunity to blossom, or if it causes him to snub the opportunity, the Cosmos does not hold the lover responsible to rescue the relationship. The Cosmos is generous and fair. If the one who has been disappointed remains true to himself, the Cosmos will bless him with a relationship that even more truly suits him. This help of the Cosmos has been observed by many people who, after being unfairly dismissed from their employment, suddenly are offered the "ideal job."

Loyalty to their inner truth leads each partner to grow deep roots of trust in the other's integrity. This trust, in turn, becomes a natural loyalty that guards each partner's feelings from the more subtle invasions and challenges that are offered by both their egos, such as satiation. It is one of the ego's characteristics to indulge in feelings of satiation when things are going well.

Satiation is an ego-based emotion that arises just when everything has been going smoothly, and the relationship has been blessed with success. It is as yet another form of vanity, the ego's claiming that it has been responsible for everything's going right. Among the hexagrams that particularly warn us about the dangers of satiation are Hexs. 11, 19, and 63, although many others also make reference to it.

Satiation often happens, for example, after the sexual climax. The ego, displaced prior to the couple's meeting in the act of love, reenters afterward as a feeling of self-sufficiency, or even a discontented mood. Many men, for example, report that in the climax of sexual intercourse they feel they have lost something of themselves. Denis De Rougemont describes this in his *Love in the Western World* (Princeton University Press, 1940) as a "death experience." What was lost in this case is the ego, which has momentarily died. This death is similar to what happens in shock: the ego becomes temporarily inoperative, but the true self that has become attached to the ego thinks it has lost a part of itself.

Women experience satiation too, but more as an ebullient self-confidence. In both cases, the satiated feeling is expressed in the thought that the other is not as important as one supposed, or if there have been difficulties, the thought, "Why am I enduring this difficult relationship?" Such ego-based moods of false independence tempt one to become disloyal to one's inner truth, and therefore to discard one's natural loving feelings to the other's true self, or to restlessly want more from the relationship, or even to look for more desirable mates. The *I Ching* calls this "joyousness that is weighed" in Hex. 58, Line 4, meaning that one allows the ego to weigh what it "prefers." Such weighing causes one to forget one's inner relationship with the beloved. If satiation, and the ego behind it, is not perceived and stopped at the outset, the lover's access to his inner connection becomes blocked, and he no longer nourishes the other as before. The love thus becomes a one-way street where one partner robs the other of love's chi energy.

Still another problem related to satiation is the feeling many people have that when they feel warm toward their partner, the partner becomes distant and unloving; then when they give up on him and start to move away, the partner suddenly shows loving interest. This is typical of the ego-based feeling of satiation. The one exhibiting satiation is arrogantly indulging in feelings of self-sufficiency. This arrogance quickly disappears when the other retreats, because once more this person is forced to acknowledge his interdependency. Allowing this pattern to repeat itself over and over is dangerous, since the one hurt and frustrated may one day really give up. The remedy is to keep aware so that when we feel restless, we remind ourselves of our interdependency. If the problem lies in the other, it is necessary to withdraw until he recognizes what he is doing.

Another form of satiation has its roots in the patriarchal attitude that can be observed in many marriages, namely, that if a woman is not properly submissive, the husband has not become the man he should be to fulfill his position of dominance. Yet when his wife is submissive, he feels that she truly is inferior, and that he, therefore, is stuck with a loser. In this situation, both lose self-esteem. He really needs her to be strong and equal, but the patriarchal system makes a man ashamed of a strong and equal woman. Thus, the submissiveness of the wife may cause the husband to seek outside affairs that release him from this conflict. The remedy is to recognize that the problem is rooted in satiation and inequality, and to deal with it promptly through saying a firm inner No to it.

Finally, loyalty must be distinguished from what society calls loyalty, but means possession. Possessiveness in the relationship is due to the ego, and its false claims in one partner to having rights to the loving feelings of the other. It is due to this kind of possessiveness that the children from a former marriage may not be welcomed by the stepparent. If a person is loyal to his inner truth, he will respect the ties the beloved has with his children, friends, and family, and not interfere with them. Loyalty to his inner truth will prevent the other from feeling embarrassed that he comes with children, friends, and family. If one perceives that the other is making mistakes in dealing with these other relationships, it will be out of respect and not loyalty that he leaves these matters to his partner.

Loyalty is also confused with thinking one has the duty to have feelings of love when one does not have them, and the duty to stay together even though no inner connection exists, or the inner connection has been cut off. All such ideas of loyalty are actually betrayal of the person's inner truth.

Justice

Naturally, if either begins the relationship with a list of capricious demands based on vanity, such as what his family, community, society, or tradition requires, the difficulties at the beginning will be great and long-lasting, since neither can submit with dignity to capricious demands. Meeting halfway means meeting justly. One's requirements are confined only to the most essential things, things that anyone, anywhere, on looking into his heart, can agree to be just and fair.

Fairness, like kindness, is an original quality of the true self, but it becomes sullied when we gradually allow it to give way to indifference. Fairness means that we are willing to do our fair share of the work involved in relating.

During the difficulty at the beginning, limits must be set. This means that both lovers need to be aware of times when the other's ego attempts to get away with injustices and inequities, or tries to dominate. It is necessary to recognize these violations the minute they occur, to say an inner No, and then turn the matter over to the Cosmos for correction. The lover being transgressed upon must not be tempted to gloss over the problem. Inequities become established only because one of the partners is not inwardly firm about what is correct. Once a person has made this determination, and has become resolved that he shall not allow within himself any weakness or doubt about what is fair (equal, reciprocal, sensitive), he lets go of the issue. Then he trusts the other to see and correct his mistake. In the meantime, he inwardly withdraws to give the other the space needed to recognize his mistake and make the correction.

We create openings for others to transgress when we are not sure of our position. Lack of clarity about what is correct enables others' egos to sense these holes in our personality and leads them to test, to see what our boundaries are. People who cheat often rely on creating confusion in our minds by pretending, for example, that we gave a $5 bill instead of a $100 bill. When we are absolutely sure of what we have done, the cheat backs down. Similarly, when we are absolutely firm in our minds about what is just and correct, people do not test us.

It is important, while setting limits, that one not fix the beloved as a problem person, or as defective in any way, but simply as one who has made the mistake of encroaching, and that the situation has offered the opportunity to set the correct limits.

Reciprocity

Reciprocity, as already noted, is one of the most essential elements in the love relationship. Without it, the circuit of energy that is love remains incomplete. A relationship can limp along, but Hex. 54, Line 2, compares the one who is denied reciprocity to a "one-eyed man who is able to see." The commentary continues, "Here the situation is that of a girl married to a man who has disappointed her. Man and wife ought to work together like a pair of eyes. Here the girl is left behind in loneliness; the man of her choice either has become unfaithful or has died." The fourth line of this hexagram further counsels us that it is better to wait for the correct person to come along than to compromise the essentials of love. Line 3 of this hexagram compares one who gives himself, while reciprocity is missing, to a slave who has sold his dignity to satisfy his desires.

Two people can be in love with one another on the inner plane without that love being fully reciprocated on the outer plane. If a relationship becomes externalized while this situation exists, one of them has compromised the essential requirement of reciprocity. Women often allow this to happen by accepting that they should be submissive. They give without receiving because that is expected by patriarchal tradition. This devotion is misguided, for it is wrong to accept that the other shall withhold his love, or that a partial love is better than none. Such a person does not trust that by being firm in his values, the other will willingly give his love and respect. More importantly, such a person does not trust the other to grow enough to understand and accept what is correct. Such distrust guarantees failure.

To truly love another, it is necessary to see that one's love has the greater purpose of helping the beloved to grow, and that this can only be achieved by withdrawing into reserve, trusting the other to figure things out for himself. This is necessary until the other's "little boy" or "little girl" attitude gives way. Each will need to search his attitude to see whether he holds back his love while expecting that the other be devoted and giving of himself. Each will need to see whether he is in the habit of giving without requiring that the other give back, thus allowing and cultivating in the other a spoiled attitude.

If the lover allows such an imbalance, he will only experience depression, exhaustion, and sickness. The *chi* energy achieved through reciprocity in love is essential food for the body and psyche. Without it they sicken, and the will to live that is essential to health, dies. Reciprocity is absolutely essential in relationships.

Equality

Again, because of patriarchal tradition, equality between men and women is absent in many relationships. A major reason for the dominance of one partner over the other is that this tradition continues to this day unquestioned, and is the main role model available.

Equality, however, is the hallmark of the truly loving relationship. It must be established before either accepts being comfortable with the other, otherwise inequality will always be a source of conflict that will manifest as competition and envy, rather than as the cooperation that is natural to love.

That either should dominate over the other must be regarded as unacceptable. This issue can and should be settled at the very beginning by a firm decision on the part of the one who is being expected to yield. Love is a mutual respect, each for the other's space, and each for the other's ability to guide himself.

When one seeks to enforce dominance, the other must retreat into reserve. The one retreating continues to be friendly, and sometimes even close, but only when the ground is level between them. When the dominant one tests, as by seeking to intimidate, the other must not acquiesce inwardly, but withdraw into reserve. He becomes neutral, and waits until the other has recognized his error and has returned to treating him with respect. He does not hold out for apologies, or for promises to change, but simply responds, opening again when the other is sincere, and retreating if he falls back into an egocentric, arrogant attitude. In following this path of gentle disengagement, no barriers are created between them.

Often the one who has encroached will feel ashamed and humiliated, without showing it. His humiliation will prevent him from being able to move toward unity. Then, if our intuition approves, it is good to meet him with gentleness. In making such a move, it is important that we do not go too far by trying to do his work of meeting halfway for him. We merely make the opening for him to come forward on his own.

Disengagement is a special attitude. It is like the fax machine that is constantly ready to receive messages. It is on neutral alert, neither anticipating nor shut off. It is a non-directed, open receptivity in which one's mental attention is not focused on the other's outer actions. The heart, on the other hand, is kept open and loving, connected with the other's true self.

The ego's ultimate challenge comes with the threat, during the difficulty at the beginning, to break off the relationship. The one challenged must not react fearfully, but recognize the source of the threat, and say a firm inner No to it, and again, turn the matter over to the Cosmos. Where a true connection of the heart exists, there is also the potential for correction.

Another challenge may come as flattery. The one seeking to dominate may hope to lure the other into a comfortable abandonment of his reserve before a true equality has been established. If the one thus challenged gives way before a sincere equality has been achieved, he will not only have compromised his principles, he will have set the ground for future problems.

All challenges for dominance can be met by saying an inner No to the other's ego-behavior, and by remaining reserved until the challenging ceases, and until the other sees, with insight and humility, both his own spoiled demands, and the beloved's true value and worth. While the one being challenged maintains reserve, he neither complains nor attempts to change the situation; he leaves it up to the other to sense the cause of the obstruction, and to deal with it. Saying an inner No is not passive, but what the *I Ching* refers to as "undertakings that bring good fortune," and being "firm and correct.'" If one is not inwardly firm, the inner weakness will be perceived by the other's ego and even be taken as permission to continue. An outer battle against another's ego cannot be won, for egos cannot be wrestled down. Furthermore, because such attempts come from one's own ego, one falls out of harmony with the Cosmos and loses its support. The ego can only be undermined by a steadfast adherence to one's values and sense of truth, which, because it is in harmony with the Cosmos, draws its support and help. (See Hex. 43, commentary to the Judgment.)

Often the one seeking to dominate does so because his ego has convinced him that he is in some way unequal to his partner. His ego may create in him the fear that because the other is inwardly firm, he will end in being dominated. When faced with another's insecurity, or sense of inferiority, it is necessary to give him time and space to see that there is nothing of this sort to fear, and to allow his distrust to gradually dissolve through experiencing that his boundaries are consistently respected. Whenever envy is involved, however, it is always necessary to firmly reject it with an inner No.

Equality also means equal responsibility, both to disengage and to welcome the other back when they become open. While neither glosses over the other's unequal treatment, to ingratiate himself, when corrections have been made, they greet each other fully and lovingly, without holding back in an indolent, unforgiving indifference.

Often, once a relationship has been established, one of the partners will begin to turn over to the other various aspects of his responsibility for himself, such as the care of his body, and the responsibility for his self-development. This always happens as a trade-off of some sort, by which his ego perceives that a deal has been made, and he is getting the best of it. But in all such trades there is a price to pay, since the way of the Cosmos is to be responsible for oneself. The expression among women that, "The way to a man's heart is through his stomach" is an example of the sort of manipulation by which a woman may seek to dominate through cultivating the man's appetites and weaknesses. The man may see through this, but will allow it through laziness. Such trades of unmanly and unwomanly dependence are the legacy of the patriarchal tradition. They are always made at the expense of growth and truth. The help each gives the other, and their generosity toward each other, can safely be given only when, and so long as, each has "delicacy of feeling" toward the other. Then there is no loss of self, or harm (see Hex. 41, Lines 1 and 6).

In the same way, it is incorrect to try to take over another's responsibility for himself, for in so doing, we prepare him to find another to do it for him once we tire of the burden. Therefore, we should avoid supervising and lifeguarding our partners, for lifeguarding is a kind of distrust that not only undermines their self-esteem, but gives them the false impression that they may safely swim with the sharks because we are watching out for them. When one sees the beloved making serious mistakes, one should cease looking at him with one's inner eye. It is better to turn away and go one's way, having confidence that the other will find his way out of the danger. As it is written in Hex. 52, Line 2, "One cannot rescue him whom one follows." By turning a person's life entirely over to him, he quickly sees that he is alone in his dangerous diversions.

Finally, although many people think that love is a willing acceptance of the beloved's burdens, such burdens will finally overwhelm the free-willed love relationship. Equality as responsibility for oneself is essential.

When equality is in place, neither partner encourages feelings of servility or superiority in the other. Each person will be developed more in some areas than the other. If one shows more capability, he should not use it to prove that he is superior or special, or to competitively undermine the other. This does not mean that he must deny or hide his abilities, but rather that he will not allow himself to adopt a superior attitude. He will keep his inner attitude equal, and remain aware of the unique qualities the other has that match and complement him perfectly, even though they may not be of such a tangible or directly measurable nature.

It is also wise, in the totally free relationship, to recognize that each partner will fail, from time to time, in observing the essentials of relating. Each time this happens, we need to recognize the error, say an inner No to it, and then let go of it. The more we hold on to it with worry, the more the other's ego will feel embarrassed and relate to us in a negative way.

When the other makes a mistake, it is best if we do not allow ourselves to react with irritation and impatience, but wait until the beloved's true self reemerges. In the meantime, we keep a moderate attitude. To do this, we need only remember how difficult it has been to keep ourselves disciplined. We therefore recognize that the other will err, even as we ourselves have erred. We allow him to find his own way, even as we need his patience when we are searching to find our way. And, we allow that he will need at times to make mistakes, in order to learn. Meanwhile, we keep the door to our heart open and ready for his return. Such patience and perseverance, both with the other and with ourselves, is the work of love.

It is impossible for any two people to be well-enough developed at the beginning to proceed as indicated in these pages. If we are sincere in our way of life, the deficiencies of either partner will be of no great consequence. (See Hex. 14, Line 5.) All that is needed is a sincere effort on both their parts to follow their inner truth. One partner will be, at different times, more in touch with his inner truth than the other. He needs to retain his humility, so that the feelings of inequality that result from erring can dissolve in the humility of understanding.

Patience

At first glance, one might gather from the passivity traditionally associated as being the *I Ching* "way," that it counsels a person to endlessly put up with whatever ego behavior occurs in others. In fact, for a long time I took this as its meaning, and persevered with endless patience. In part, this was due to a Chinese character that Wilhelm translated as "perseverance," but which the Oxford sinologist Legge translated as "firm and correct." Shortly after writing the first edition of this book, I realized that the way we are meant to deal with incorrect behavior in others and in ourselves is to say an inner No to it, and this is often the meaning of "perseverance" and being "firm and correct." I was to clearly learn that we are not meant to patiently endure others' insensitivity, encroachment, or other mistreatment. Indeed, at times when others are abusing us openly, an outer No is required as well. The subject of this section has to do more with impatience as ego behavior. Impatience often comes from feeling we have no way to influence difficult or incorrect situations. The person who believes this is simply unaware that he can have an enormous effect by saying the inner No, turning the matter over to the Cosmos, and asking for its help.

Lovers' inner connections with each other become blocked when they allow themselves to fall prey to impatience. This happens when we fasten our attention in a negative way on external things that have happened. We allow the happening to fall into an old, grooved way of routing information through the mind.

Impatience comes with such automatic routing. When something we are working for does not happen, the item is automatically commandeered by the supervising ego that then calls up all sorts of complaints and disparaging thoughts. This spoiled pattern is played over and over again, until we rebuild our desktop to bypass the ego's old routings.

Impatience occurs because of previously set parameters in the mind regarding the time-frame in which things should happen. These parameters are reasonable to the straight-line logic of the ego, but in the dynamics of free-willed relationships, such ego demands and expectations have no place. Most problematic are those demands that are based on the older, patriarchal system of fixed, legalized relationships, in which people are given rights and duties, and where willing consent does not need to be waited for. "You owe this to me," is the expression of righteous, impatient expectation. Expectations, rights, duties, and the inevitable blame that follows them, destroy love. When the relationship has been set on a correct foundation, and each knows his limits, each also knows and recognizes the other's great value. Through this appreciation and care, neither allows himself to fall into the luxurious apathy of not observing the essentials of relating. Instead of trying to avoid them, they will want to perform them as a way of expressing their love for each other.

Impatience always belies the presence of the ego in the background, seeking to dominate. Impatience is a statement of disbelief that if we do not try to force the relationship, it will never get anywhere. It is weakness inasmuch as we will allow ourselves to want the other while his ego is still in charge. Impatience would either encourage us to become a slave to our desires, or to discard the relationship because it is troublesome. Either kind of impatience only strengthens the other's ego, causing it to hold out for dominance. Only when the other sees that under no circumstances will we sell our dignity short, will he deal with his ego, since all our strengths and weaknesses are communicated to him through the inner channel.

Although impatience is often followed by things getting better, we find that in the end we have achieved very little. What has been achieved is offset by the increase it brings to our own ego, for then we find that we have a slightly turned-off attitude because we have waited so long, and have only achieved very little. To the ego small progress is never enough, therefore impatience only grows. The ego is never satisfied. Soon the turned-off attitude that simulates inner independence, but which really is a deluded self-confidence, turns to a careless indifference and resentment. It is then followed by feelings of isolation, because the ego always isolates us from the Cosmic harmony. Sometimes this pattern needs to be repeated several times before we are able to see with absolute clarity that impatience, and the ego pressure that creates it, must go. In Hex. 44, Line 1, impatience is pictured as a lean pig that once fed, rages around. This image shows the truly demonic nature of the ego.

Because the inner channel between the two lovers is so direct, each perceives any hint of impatience in the other immediately, alarming his protective senses. Patience, therefore, is essential while the limits to the relationship are being established. This means that we give the other all the space he needs to find his way, and that we give ourselves the same space. Patience means loving the other wholly on the inner level, and maintaining openness by allowing no barricades or wedges to develop between our heart and theirs. On the outer level, we neither allow our ego to encroach into the other's inner space, nor theirs to encroach into ours. We constantly keep in mind, "Where there is a will, there is a way," allowing the other to find the will, all by himself to meet us halfway. The *I Ching* talks about attaining another's "willing consent." Specifically, this means not bribing, pushing, urging, or doing his half of the work. Meeting halfway can happen only as the other becomes more conscious of his deep inner love, which grows in a direct ratio to his growing respect for our loyalty to our own true feelings. This loyalty to our true selves is what is communicated through the inner connection.

Humility

Humility is another essential of the love relationship. Without humility, one tends to encroach into the other's space, or to be impatient when mistakes are made. Humility, surely, is the foundation of all other natural virtues.

A priest member of Alcoholics Anonymous was quoted as saying, "It is through being humiliated that we learn humility." It is by going through the difficulties of setting ourselves in order, that we are able to bear with the deficiencies of others. Mutual stumbling makes lovers aware of their mutual humanity. This awareness, in turn, deepens their love into a lasting bond with each other.

In the absence of true humility, which is the source of spontaneous affection, the love relationship dries up. Pride and vanity can exist in a relationship that sets itself up for public approval, but love will suffer.

We regain humility when the ego's pretenses have either been decreased through shock and adversity, or through having been consciously relinquished. Such a person has looked at himself squarely and realized his true place in the Cosmos: that while he is unique, he is not special. His self-respect comes from recognizing the very gift of his life, and that this gift is undermined whenever he adopts pretenses about himself. Thus he no longer needs to pretend he is more than others, while realizing also that he is not less, either. He realizes that all pretenses of being better are but the delusion and vanity of the ego. Recognizing his own true nature, he is also able to recognize others' true natures, therefore he does not need to play up or down to anyone. While not being deceived by other's pretenses, he does not challenge or resist them because he knows the pretenses exist without the other's being aware of them. He knows why and how they are there, and so does not use that as yet one more excuse to conclude he is better.

We regain humility is often thought of as passively accepting poverty and lowliness. From the Cosmic viewpoint humility is being free of the fear of not having enough, and of not being enough, in and of oneself. It is a trust that if one is sincere in one's way of life, and in harmony with the Cosmos, everything that one undertakes will receive its help to have enough. The ego, which is based on the fear of not having enough, drives a person to be self-assertive, competitive, and possessive, always in search of getting more. Enough is never enough, and even though the person, by following his ego, may attain great wealth and position, he can only do so at the expense of his true self.

It is essential, in the love relationship, and no less so in the bodily expression of love, not to indulge the ego by building up vanity, especially as sexual prowess, or as feelings of self-importance. Sexuality is truly fulfilling only when it comes from feelings of love. When a person's vanity becomes centered in his sexuality, it becomes an instrument of the ego, used by it compulsively for self-gratification, and to possess and dominate others. No longer the humble, earthy form that attains its sublimity through love, the true nature of sexuality is slandered. It is necessary, always, to be conscientious not to allow love to become imprisoned in a sexuality that is indulged in for its own sake.

The *I Ching* regards sexuality as the ornament of love , the way the beard is an ornament of the chin. It says, "To devote care to it for its own sake, without regard for the inner content of which it is an ornament, would bespeak a certain vanity" (Hex. 22, Line 2). Often the ego, doubting that love will ever be externalized, impatiently tries to make it happen, by forcing feelings out into the open. Such attempts only obstruct love because the gift of love can come only when we keep it free of ego interference. The correct attitude is to treasure it when it comes, let go of it when it goes, and keep it free by not expecting or demanding it as a right. Love is inextricably bound up with this sort of modesty.

Sensitivity

Sensitivity is probably the most important essential of relating. It is at the heart of the free-willed love relationship.

One might say, of course, that if people are in love, sensitivity exists, that it is the very nature of love. Nevertheless, true sensitivity is an awareness that needs to be distinguished from the definition the ego gives it, which is an expectation that we should respect its pride system, as when people think we are "insensitive" because we have withdrawn from their egos.

Sensitivity is a careful conscientiousness to keep aware of certain things. For example, although we have won a place in the other's private inner space, we never presume we are more than a guest there. We remain forever without entitlements and rights, either to be insensitive, or to tell the other what is wrong with him, what he should or should not do, what friends he may have, or any other such invasions into his private feelings or thoughts. Sensitivity also means that one does not presume on the other, either on his good feelings, his trust in us, his willingness to help us, or his devotion to us. We remain careful of these invaluable assets of our relationship, guarding them with humility, gratitude, and respect.

A dream that occurred while this chapter was being written clarified this subject even further:

In New York City, I had gone to a small upstairs restaurant to eat. (In real life, I had been to a similar restaurant run by a woman who had developed a select clientele for her gourmet

Brazilian meals.) The restaurant of my dream was run by two women who also relied on word-of-mouth for their customers.

The women offered me two or three dishes that together reminded me of a soup I once had in Paris that was quite delicious. My mention of this experience seemed to suggest to them that they make an all-vegetable soup. They said, because I was the only guest at that moment, they would wheel out a special table and prepare the soup in front of me, so I could see how it was made.

What particularly caught my attention was the careful and loving way they went about putting the meal together. As they finally put the soup in the dish, adding garnishes in an artful way, they placed the dish before me, smiling and pleased, as if they were saying, "Voila!"

The taste was marvelous, indescribable. As I ate, my body felt nourished and invigorated.

The three of us seemed to chat pleasantly, and they seemed as delighted in my enjoyment as I was, relishing the soup. For an instant, I thought of saying that had I known how the soup in Paris had been prepared, I would have appreciated it so much more. But then I realized that talking about that soup of another time would thoughtlessly distract from the beauty of this moment, so I said nothing. As I finished, one of them was called away by the doorbell to the downstairs entrance. In another minute she returned and replied, to the inquiring expression of her partner, that she had rejected the customer. She only said, "I could tell that he was unfeeling." The other woman immediately acknowledged this as a correct reason not to cook for him.

Immediately upon awaking, the significance of the dream was revealed in the word "feeling," which seemed to pronounce itself particularly. Then it immediately became apparent that the sensitivity that is essential to the love relationship is really delicacy of feeling, the tender consideration for the other that this dream indicated. To love another is to have feeling for him.

Forgiveness

From the *I Ching* point of view, forgiveness is one of those pomposities in which the ego indulges to make itself feel superior. In the oblique way that the *I Ching* teaches, it is just when a person has thought he has sacrificed his pride to forgive another, that he receives Hexagram 63, Line 5, which says, "The neighbor in the east who slaughters an ox does not attain as much real happiness as the neighbor in the west with his small offering." The commentary mentions the "magnificence" of the large offering, giving us a clue as to the Cosmic meaning behind this metaphor. Indeed, the whole business of sacrifice is thrown into question, regardless of whether it is a large or a small offering.

One learns through experience that the word "misfortune" mentioned in many lines of the *I Ching*, indicates that disharmonious acts create an adverse Cosmic reaction we call fate, and that it is the business of fate to return the evil deed to its doer in the manner of a boomerang. This actually happens if no one interferes. Fate restores the Cosmic harmony while making the person reflect and correct himself. The act of forgiveness on the part of humans is an interference and false magnificence that also creates a fate for the one who does it. The only need for any forgiveness is to forgive oneself, for if any feelings of blame have remained after correcting oneself, such self-blaming activity comes from the ego that likes to attach itself to mistakes we have made. From the Cosmic point of view, correcting oneself frees one from both blame and fate.

The ego also likes to blame others because blame and anger give it a sense of power. That is one of its reasons for holding grudges, the other being that it likes to instill guilt in others, to gain control over them. Allowing oneself to hold grudges strengthens the ego and weakens the true self. In this respect, the ego is a Mephistophelian element in our consciousness, ready to put forth stored up grievances the instant things go wrong. It is the ego that also blames the Cosmos that our "tedious and long perseverance" has gone unrewarded. Forgiving another, or withholding forgiveness, is another means of the ego to stay in control of the relationship, as has been explained above. The action needed is not forgiveness, but saying a strong inner No to the ego, and in meditation, to turn over to the Cosmos its list of grievances and causes for self-pity. In this way, one deprograms the ego-program running in one's psyche. The other action needed when someone is treating us insensitively is to ask the Cosmos for help to deal with the situation.

Instead of indulging in forgiveness, we need to remember that everybody has an ego. It is not merely an individual problem, but a societal one, since the false beliefs that create the ego come from the society at large. Every dastardly act is not due to the person's nature, which has been suppressed, but due to the disharmonious ideas and beliefs in his inner program. On this account, the judgments and conclusions we make about others' behavior need to be modest. Failing this modesty, we simply fall in with all the other ego behavior.

It is also important, when others feel regret for what they have done, to cleanse oneself, in meditation, of all remaining bad feelings, for allowing these feelings keeps negative vibrations flowing through the inner channel.

Chapter 10

The Work of Loving, or Establishing the Basis

Wooing, an old-fashioned word, is scarcely recognized as a concept today. Its use in the *I Ching* in connection with Hexagram 31, *Influence*, however, is cause for contemplation. One finds, through experience in consulting the *I Ching*, that wooing, in its true sense, has to do with the attraction that spontaneously and automatically occurs when we "see," with our inner eye, the true self of another person. This attraction is consistent when we are in the presence of another's true self.

Needless to say, the hexagram, in its traditional version, describes wooing quite differently, since it is one of those hexagrams that is particularly overlaid with the conventions of ancient Chinese society. It actually presents a false model of "the strong man who puts himself under the weak girl and thereby attracts her to him." Such a model is the epitome of a contrived relationship, in which courtship has the purpose of winning the girl, and when she has become his wife, to place himself on top. Such a view contradicts the principle evident in the majority of the hexagram texts, that harmony can never come from contrivance but only from being in touch with one's inner truth.

The underlying meaning of this hexagram has to do with the influence our thoughts and feelings automatically have on others and on things—*the hidden and constant influence of consciousness.* This and other hexagrams indicate that all consciousness influences things, even to the point of influencing the way things behave. In view of the findings of modern science, this is not surprising. Atomic physicists were among the first to observe that the behavior of atomic particles was influenced by the scientists who were observing them. These, and other experiments have caused today's scientists to conclude that "the object of research cannot be separated from the researcher."

Throughout, the *I Ching* makes us aware that the "hidden causes" of things have to do with the effects produced by the way we think about them. It calls this the "inner truth" of the situation, which we cannot understand, merely by observing externals. Consulting the *I Ching* allows us to intercept and perceive this inner truth. Early in my own work with the *I Ching,* I learned that my doubts and negative thoughts were not simply passive things, but had an active, destructive effect. The entire point made again and again, and which has been the very basis of the *I Ching* is that when a person is inwardly in harmony with the Cosmos, he draws its help and blessings, whether it be to change a situation, to be protected from harm, to obtain his needs, or to find the way back to health. When we are not in harmony within ourselves, we are outside the greater harmony of the Cosmos. Being in harmony, we further learn, does not have to do with our actions, but with the innermost thoughts that give rise to those actions.

What then is this system of harmony I here call "the Cosmos?" As I have learned from the *I Ching* in the years since this book was first published, the entire Cosmos is consciousness. This also means that all the things we see in the material world are aspects that have manifested out of that consciousness into the compressed forms we call "reality." The compressed forms represent the visible world of Nature. Their experiences feed into the overall Cosmic consciousness in the same way a person's body cells feed into the person's overall awareness that we call his conscious mind, which is his invisible "part." While the person's consciousness is an aggregate of all the sensations of his cells, it is in no way separate from those cells which constitute the visible aspect of himself. It is in precisely the same way that we and everything that exists contributes to the aggregate awareness of the Cosmic consciousness.

The *I Ching* further makes us aware that the Cosmic consciousness, like our feeling consciousness at birth, is totally wholesome and good. It is the very system of harmony that feeds and nourishes what Lao Tzu called "the ten-thousand things of existence." It becomes clear, when our picture of reality begins to include both the visible and the invisible worlds, that "everything is consciousness." It is because of this that our individual thoughts and feelings play a great role in our relationships, and in our lives in general. The Chinese realized in ancient times that the Cosmos is a system of harmony that excludes all discord. The use of the words "success" and "misfortune," used in the texts of nearly every hexagram line, have to do with whether what we are thinking, doing, or planning is in harmony with the Cosmic harmony, or not. Indeed, it is our thoughts that determine the outcome.

Seeing how we are so intimately connected with the Cosmos, we can then understand how love, the energy of attraction that holds the entire Cosmos together, and which is also our "life force," is not simply something that happens between two people, all by themselves. At some point in our lives, often during times when we have been separated from the Cosmic unity, love enters, as I have expressed earlier, as a Cosmic gift which is both an opportunity and a challenge. It is a gift, as it is put in Hex. 29, Line 4, "handed through the window," to help us put our lives back on course, to help us grow, and to do so in the happiest and most wonderful way possible. Indeed, it is there to help us realize the kind of Cosmos it is, and to help us rid ourselves of the slanders that have been laid upon it, upon Nature, and indeed, upon our own natures.

The first edition of this book tried to describe the difficulties that surround the beginning of the love relationship, to enable lovers to find ways of overcoming the entry-level problems that would prevent the love relationship from happening, or else ruin it swiftly afterwards. Wooing described that period before the relationship became established. Today, after recognizing even more keenly the power of thought, both negative and positive, I prefer to see the beginning in less negative terms because I have realized that as we presume things to be, so they become. I prefer to see beginnings in the more positive description of "making a new beginning."

Wooing as I here use the term, is not the pursuit of the beloved, as the word is normally used. It is an activity by which the basis for loving is established, through following one simple rule: to allow the love energy to flow to the beloved when, *and only when,* he is acting from his true self. Here, I refer to those times when the true self is not being obstructed by the ego; that means when the true self is in the seat of consciousness. Then, there is sensitivity, and the willingness to extend trust. There are no competitive games of one-upmanship being played, no jokes at the other's expense, no indulgence in self-pity, no encroachments into his private space, no possessiveness, no insistence on following convention, and all the other types of activities described in this book, in which the ego likes to indulge. The sincerity and modesty by which one can know the true self is there, are always something one can feel as wholesome and good. If any other strange feeling is mixed in, it can indicate that the ego is trying to simulate these qualities in order to get something it does not deserve, and which it will ultimately use against the other.

It is important to remember where love comes from, for when a person is not in harmony with himself, he begins to shut off his connection with its source. Love comes from the Cosmos and courses through the two lovers to complete a circuit. The Cosmos is the essential "third party" that needs to be consciously included in the relationship. The fact that the love comes from the Cosmos means that we also have a certain responsibility not to throw love away on the ego. Forgetting the source and our responsibility to it is like shutting off a fountain. We also need to realize that the Cosmos can supply us with the love energy, whether we have a love partner or not. All of our social training, by making us believe a partner is necessary, causes us to take partners without regard to whether there is an inner connection.

Wooing is the activity of controlling the flow of love from our hearts. Having said this, it is vital to add that if we allow the ego to be in control of this activity, a fate is created. The ego would use love as a power device to get something from the other, to tyrannize over him, or to control his behavior. Giving love to get has definite penalties connected with it, for all such intentions transmit through the love channel as negative energy.

Wooing means one thing only: withdrawing one's love energy in the face of the other's ego, and reopening the heart when his true self is present. The withdrawal is into an inner neutrality which is like a car in neutral gear. It neither moves forward nor backward. No effort is put into any motion at all. Withdrawal is felt by the other, but not as immediately as the renewal of love energy is felt. While the other is in the fullness of his ego, the feeling of loss enters more like a wedge. It is scarcely felt at first, but enough to make a slight halting in the ego's output. No sooner is it noticed on the feeling plane than it becomes conscious as a feeling of decrease. This awareness continues until it replaces the bravado of the ego with a clear feeling of loss and abandonment. The message that is sent is not intercepted or read by the other's ego, but is read by his true self. It stops his allowing the ego and his relying on it, and it causes him to see (1) that something is going wrong, and (2) that the seeming success of his ego is not working in his interest. This causes him speedily to remove his full support of the ego. When withdrawal is combined with a consciously said inner No, it causes his true self to stop his ego altogether.

Return to the true self happens gradually. The person is not always sure that he can dispense with his ego, therefore the ego hangs around, to see if there is a new opening. For this reason, despite a beginning improvement in the situation, it is important to hold back in reserve until the true self has really stayed in place. The message that his ego is not to be allowed becomes more clearly understood when we reopen our heart to him. Wooing consists of practicing this way of relating until the point is secure and the ego is not allowed back in. These principles of relating apply to all relationships, the way we relate to tempers in children, the way we relate to problems in business, and so on, except that in these latter situations, the energy we give is not this intimate kind of love. It is an open-heartedness we extend to them.

The *I Ching* calls this kind of relating "advancing with the openings, and retreating with the closings." Wooing is the consistent practice of responding to people from this principle.

It cannot be emphasized enough, in view of the subtleties by which the ego would like to seize this kind of action and use it as a power, that to woo means first disallowing one's own ego. In whatever way we use love as a device, we not only fall out of the Cosmic harmony, we damage the love relationship. Wooing, it needs to be made clear, cannot be to achieve a purpose. To do something to make another thing happen is to be purposeful. Wooing is to retreat from doing something disharmonious such as throwing our love away on another's ego. We simply and only act from our own integrity to protect that integrity. The fact that it has a result in the real world shows the interconnectedness of inner work and its manifestation on the visible plane. It shows us as well aspects of the way the Cosmos works.

We need to realize that when the ancient Chinese observed the workings of fate, they came to wrong conclusions about its purpose. For example, they experienced the withdrawal of the Cosmic protection and concluded that they were being punished. Thus, some hexagrams speak about misfortune (fate) as punishments, whereas, what they are really referring to are Cosmic "corrections." The work of loving, in that it involves this kind of withdrawing, leads to the person's correcting himself, rather than one's correcting him. The advantage of correcting a situation in this way is that it takes place outside the awareness of the other's ego, it does not involve our own ego, and it avoids the hateful effects created when outer action and reproaches cause a loss of face.

The basis of loving, then, is correctly responding. It is always responding, rather than initiating action. We respond to where the other is within himself. To a certain extent this requires that we have a knowledge of the way the Cosmos works, but it is sufficient, within the confines of this book, that we realize it is a system of harmony from which all discordant ideas and thoughts are excluded. As mentioned before, our true natures are in harmony with the Cosmos but our egos are not. Inasmuch as we cultivate the ego either in ourselves or others, we fall out of the Cosmic consciousness. Furthermore, those thoughts and attitudes which are discordant create fates for ourselves.

Fate, which is referred to in so many lines of the *I Ching* as "misfortune," means the unpleasant events that result from disharmonious thoughts and acts. The purpose of fate is to cause us to reflect and correct ourselves. Unpleasant events and feelings of loneliness tell us we are not connected with the greater Cosmic unity. We need to realize that it is not the Cosmos that has abandoned us, but we who have abandoned it. Fate, the *I Ching* also tells us, is always ended when we correct ourselves.

One of the common mistakes lovers make due to conventional beliefs is thinking that the love they experience comes from the partner. They do not realize that it comes *through* the partners as the physical vehicles for that love. They often do not realize that love is a gift from the Cosmos, and that they are not its source. No one can make love happen. It is given with the purpose of awakening, developing and freeing their true selves from the dominance of their egos. It is given to help them realize that they exist in a much greater matrix from which they have shut themselves off by seeing themselves as the special creatures of creation. While each human being is a *unique* aspect of the Cosmic whole, every other aspect is also unique, and therefore all aspects are equal to each other. The exalted view humans have adopted of themselves as being "special" has caused them to lose their modesty, and with it, the Cosmic gifts that come in abundance to those who are modest. Such modesty has nothing to do with the self-image of being a modest person, or with any ideas that see modesty as equaling poverty or selflessness, which is really self-denial. Love alone has the potential to reawaken their awareness of their true relationship with the Cosmos.

Understanding these Cosmic principles, it is possible for the lovers to establish the basis of loving. It requires that they reject the models of relationship they have learned, in which one of the lovers is expected to have the role of dominance, the other to have the role of submissiveness. These roles have nothing to do with peoples' true natures, or with the true nature of relationships. What they are consistent with are the models of feudal social organization that have existed over all the world, and are even the basis of democracies. Feudalism is a pyramidal hierarchy in which the authority of the individual over himself is taken away from him by society at birth, and transferred to his parents, who are put up over him; this authority, as he grows older, then gets transferred to others higher and higher on. The belief that one needs to be authorized by society in everything one does gives rise to the models of acceptable behavior mentioned above. As they are based on the disrespect for the individual's authority over himself, they can be seen to be the source of endless problems in the love relationship. For example, the person who sees himself in the submissive role follows the model of enduring and tolerating the other's ego in exchange for being taken care of emotionally. The one in the dominant role views himself as free to do whatever he sees fit, and as having the right to act from his ego. In time, the one in the submissive role either grows beyond the narrow confines of dependence, or remains suffering within an inner house that is too small to move about in. In time, the one in the dominant role begins to despise the other for his emotional dependence and lack of self-sufficiency. These roles have been defined erroneously as reflecting a "natural polarity." They are simply and only roles borrowed from the 3,000 year old social behavior inherited from feudalism.

The existence of such roles cause the one with the dominant role to fear the other, believing that he will be engulfed in his dependency. The one with the submissive role constantly fears that he will be abandoned, and so only increases his possessiveness as the other withdraws into a more independent and indifferent stance. The work of love is to become liberated from these role models in which their egos are invested.

Liberation from decadent roles requires a continuous process of deprogramming. This means discovering the words, phrases, and images which make up the programs, and saying a firm and strong inner No to them, and to every rationale which has been formulated to keep these images installed as an inner program. The only way the two lovers can discover and fulfill their uniqueness is to zap these false inner programs.

One of the devices of the ego is to argue, "but then what will be left?" What is left, or rather gets uncovered, is the original program we were born with, which is adequate in every way to help us live our lives. This program still resides within us as our common sense, which often surfaces only as feelings, but also as insights. Every creative person experiences these, especially when he is empty-minded, and often while doing something totally mundane. Just then the most inventive thing, the most helpful idea, the precise way we have been seeking to resolve a problem, appears as if out of thin air. The most creative of people regard this as a special channel that has opened to them; when they have lost it, they seek over and over to find it again. That channel is their connection with their common sense, which, in turn, is in connection with the Cosmos, the source of all creative gifts.

The Cosmos, I have learned, communicates to us first through these wordless feelings. They can be tuned into. They are positive and negative, like the yang and yin lines of the *I Ching* hexagrams. They say an inner Yes to what feels harmonious and an inner No to what feels disharmonious. It is, indeed, the simple form in which the Cosmic consciousness, which is a feeling consciousness uses language. We need no other guide than this. It is simply a matter of tuning in. What keeps us from being able to tune in is the morass of preconceived ideas that fill our minds brim-full so that there is no room for the light to "come through the window." Inner emptiness makes this possible, and that is why meditation works so well for some. To make tuning in possible, we need to get rid of the programs that prevent us from feeling our feelings. The most simple of these programs contain words and expressions that discount our feelings as "silly," "unreliable," and "too simple." We need to realize that they are words that have been spoken by all the egos around us. There is hardly any child that has not been told that his feelings are not valid when it comes to judging which behavior is appropriate in a given situation. As an adult he needs to firmly reject all such slanders on his feelings, for his feelings are the Cosmic gift he has been given to tell him whether he is in harmony with his true self and the Cosmos, or not. Ridding himself of these slanders will free his access to his full range of feelings and restore his sense of being centered within himself. Fortunately, the *I Ching* is there to help him get back in touch with his feelings.

Establishing the basis for loving means to repossess our true feelings and all the other wonderful gifts we were born with, such as contact with our inner truth, and our ability to ask the Cosmos for help. They were given to us to enable us to live our lives as complete and unique beings.

Finally, the lovers need to realize that loving another is first and foremost loving and respecting themselves. This advice would be criticized by the ego as "selfish," because the ego holds "selflessness" up as a high goal. The idea of selflessness implies that our true self is considered worthy only of being thrown away. Self-respect, on the other hand, means to love and honor the Cosmic gift that our life represents. It also means taking back the authority over ourselves that we were more or less forced to transfer to others when we were very young. When the love for another comes from love and respect for oneself, it has no need for constant recognition, nor does it need to be a co-dependence. There is also no need to put the partner up or down. Respect for the other's unique needs comes from respecting one's own uniqueness and one's own needs. It also comes from respecting the uniqueness of everything that exists in the Cosmic order. When the basis for loving is correctly understood, any presence of the ego is easily recognized as a feeling of disharmony, and loss of self-esteem.

Chapter 11

The Process and Scenario of Love

In the previous chapters, reference has been made to love as having a way, course, or trajectory through which it progresses. This is referred to in this book as the "process." Progress along this trajectory occurs every time we attain the optimum mental and emotional state, that is to say, every time we are in harmony with the way the Cosmos works. This state corresponds to the way the great patterns in nature work, as for example, the course of the seasons, and the progression of one's life through several natural stages of development. The way these great patterns in nature work is called the great Tao. Likewise, when we follow the way indicated by being utterly true to ourselves, we follow our personal Tao. This puts us in harmony with the great Tao, enabling us to receive its multitudinous benefits and protection. When we are not in harmony, things grind to a standstill and progress is no longer made.

At first we gain and lose this optimum state very often, but gradually, we retain it more steadily. It is comparable to crossing a plain of pitfalls, each pit of which represents a false idea about our true natures, about the nature of the love relationship, and about the way the Cosmos works. With each inner No to a false idea that has been identified as having caused us "to fall," a pit gets filled, so that we more and more gain firm ground.

Learning to say the inner No requires awareness of what harmony feels like, and what it feels like to lose it. When we have lost it, it is time to search for the false ideas that cause the disharmony. Learning to do this requires a certain dedication and perseverance, especially at the beginning.

Getting to the optimum state of harmony, we may have been taught, is a matter of balancing ourselves, an idea that implies the human state is naturally out of balance. Balancing, then is understood as balancing a negative idea with a positive one. The optimum state of harmony, however, cannot be achieved in this way. For many years I struggled to keep my ego at bay, but always found it returning in one manner or another. Now, after learning from the *I Ching* that the ego is a complex of self-images, doubts, and fears that have become installed in the psyche as an internal program, I have also learned that it can be deprogrammed. After being thoroughly deprogrammed, the ego will try to return in small ways, but can easily be intercepted and dealt with. If not deprogrammed the negative ideas remain active in the psyche.

Just as the programs of computers are composed of words and phrases, the inner programs that comprise the various parts of the ego complex are composed of words, phrases and images. The reason they create so much trouble in the psyche is that they consist of falsehoods and half-truths that misrepresent and slander our own natures, Nature itself, and the way the Cosmos works. Some of the phrases of the program cause it to be installed, some act to keep it in place, and some act to reinstall it in case we catch on to some of its falsehoods. As one big integrated program whose purpose, after convincing the true self that it is incapable and unworthy, the ego begins to work as entity that has a life of its own. In this regard, it has a demonic quality. To keep the true self disabled, it constantly puts it and its feelings down. In time, it fully succeeds in becoming the center of the personality, even speaking as "I." If outer circumstances act to support it with success, it can achieve its ultimate aim of completely replacing and extinguishing the true self. Because this is its ultimate aim, the ego is nothing less than the implacable enemy of the true self.

Precisely because it is a complex set of words, phrases, and images, it is impossible to "fight" the ego as an entity. Nevertheless, we can deprogram it, word by word, phrase by phrase, and image by image. This requires a rigorous and persistent introspection by which the phrases and images are identified. Deprogramming is achieved by reversing the original assent we have given them, whether we gave it involuntarily, as a response to threats and punishments, or we allowed them to enter simply because someone older than we said they were true, or else because they sounded "plausible" to us. By saying an inner No to each wrong word, phrase, and image with the conscious mind, we reverse our previous acceptance of them and they are removed from the inner program. This procedure may sound too simple to be believed, but it is my experience that for every word, phrase and image we have deprogrammed, the ego's power over us shrinks.

In working at this deprogramming activity with other people, I have found that people contained phrases in their psyches they were taught during childhood that they believed they had discarded years before. This fact led to the discovery that *guilt* for disbelieving the phrases had led to their being reinstalled. Guilt, I learned, is the chief means by which the ego reinstalls its programmatic phrases. Moreover, I learned that guilt has no Cosmic basis, but belongs entirely to the realm of the ego. With respect to the false program that makes up the ego, guilt has two functions: one, it acts as a lock on the basic assumptions on which the whole program is built, keeping a person from questioning those assumptions; second, it serves to reinstall, without the person's knowing, any assumptions he has come to disbelieve in. Because of these characteristics, guilt needs to be addressed as one of the first false ideas, by saying an absolutely firm inner No to it.

In doing the work of deprogramming it is important to ask for Cosmic help. The Cosmos is always ready to come to our aid to reveal the false phrases. Once a particular self-image is gone, we no longer have a need to fight its influence. By consistently deprogramming one self-image after another, we not only regain our true selves, we find our true self grows up, becoming ever stronger. By such means we regain our natural (optimum) mental and emotional state, in touch with our true inner feelings, and in harmony with our true self. The *I Ching* pictures this state, in Hex. 58, in the image of the perfectly calm lake, which mirrors everything to perfection.

The optimum state of harmony is also an attitude of gratitude toward the beneficial nature of the Cosmos. Such an attitude is the essence of modesty in the face of the Cosmic whole, of which we are all a part. This attitude will always gain an active, beneficial response from the Cosmos.

Any form of doubt of the greater unity of the Cosmos originates in the ego. Unlike the true self, the ego has no connection with the Cosmos. The ego not only envies this connection, it constantly attempts to interrupt it. When it succeeds, the personality comes into conflict, and we become out of harmony. The ensuing mental and emotional state is cloudy, confused, agitated, and even dangerous, because it is outside the protective custody of the Cosmic unity.

The Cosmic workings are always outside the understanding of the ego, with its straight-line logic and way of pursuing its goals. It sees the shortest distance between two points as being a straight line. Never mind that the line happens to go over Mt. Everest, or under the ocean. Once on a straight-line path, the ego seems oblivious of the occasional need to deviate around or over obstacles. In following this straight-line path, it creates nothing but resistance.

The way of the Cosmos, however, is the way of making progress through creating no resistances, and going around obstacles. It works solely through attraction, which succeeds through gaining a willing assent, because this is the way of love. Thus love follows a zigzag path, which we also find is the path by which the true self is developed. It is also gradual so that what is understood intellectually becomes verified by experience. Due to the obstinacy of the ego, we sometimes remain stranded in the pits of false ideas for a long time, even until those ideas drive us to the point of burnout, but once we recognize their falsehoods, we see how it was necessary to remain in those dark holes as the only way we were going to see the slanderous nature of the ideas they contained, and how we were beguiled and flattered by them. The moment we reject them, the pits get filled and we can safely continue on our way. This zigzag pattern would not be necessary at all were it not for the ego and its trickeries.

Such a path is not the flattering path of self-development pictured by the ego, as leading to the top of a mountain, or high into the clouds. It is the "path of return" mentioned by Lao Tzu, to one's true self, for the only way, once we have been lured down one of the byways of the ego, is to go back to where we left off of our true path, and continue on.

By returning from all the deviations, one engages the helpful forces of the Cosmos to make progress in all one's affairs. Attaining a steady working partnership with the Cosmos is the goal of the process. The modest recognition that we need its help puts us in harmony with it.

However, it is part of the process that we will lose the way. As Hex. 51, Line 2, says, "A hundred thousand times you lose your treasures and must climb the nine hills." Often this happens when we self-confidently think "now I have gotten rid of my ego." Such thoughts signal the very return of the ego in yet another guise. The ego is ever seeking to make us dependent on its guidance. It does this also through making us ashamed of being dependent on the Cosmos, and proclaiming the goal of a godlike independence. It achieves this through a false self-confidence behind which is the intention to say, once success comes, "I did it!" It wants to dismiss once and for all the help the person has received from the Cosmos. The Cosmos knows this aspect of the ego and withholds its aid accordingly. This false kind of self-confidence is the opposite of the inner independence we experience when we recognize, accept, and welcome our dependence on the Cosmos. Through losing the path in this and like ways, we begin to see through the devices of the ego and gradually realize in an enduring way, what it means to come into harmony with the Cosmos. Nothing is lost or wasted from having lost the way when we mine the gold that is hidden in these negative experiences.

Often during the process of gradual self-development it seems as if nothing is happening, but this is not true. During these times, the process is like an underground river that travels a long way before surfacing. Its invisibility tests our trust, but the testing only makes our trust stronger, and ourselves better able to love without needing to be important in an ego-satisfying way. Thus the strength and durability of the inner relationship is perfected.

Through following the process by taking small steps at first, one begins to see the beneficial influence on others that comes when one is in harmony with oneself.

When a person understands his part in the process, his ability to consciously acknowledge his love for the other is more enduring, and he is able to keep openhearted during the setbacks. Through disciplining his ego, he recognizes that it is the element in him that seeks to put grappling hooks into the beloved, and which urges him to press himself on the other when he has begun to retreat. Freed of the ego's influence, he is able humbly to accept love when it comes, and to let go of it when it goes. Through this humility he remains approachable, making his heart into a large house, so to speak, in which the other can live without feeling cramped.

The more dominant partner, through becoming freed of this ego-pressure, becomes able to consciously recognize his inner feelings, since there is no longer any cause for fear.

Eventually both lovers become aware that the love relationship is a wonderful vehicle to awaken them to the realization that the true self is love. This understanding frees them from the mistaken view they may have held: that life is an ongoing chaos in which the human being has been caught, by pure chance—a view that keeps today's world imprisoned in violence and chaos.

Seeing the love relationship as a process is to experience that help is always a hand's breadth away. Then we are able to flow with events, to allow the hidden purposes to be revealed, and the benefits to become manifest. In harmony with ourselves, we no longer resist the direction of our lives, but trust everything that happens as leading to where we are really meant to go.

When the lovers grasp the interrelatedness of their destinies, which often happens in retrospect, they see how everything has been part of a bigger, ongoing scenario in which beneficial and harmonious changes have replaced decadent and destructive patterns through the vehicle of time. They see that the changes happened gradually, the way petals naturally unfold into a blossom, and that self-development is the way by which the loving true self develops its uniqueness. Recognizing that changes occurring on the outer plane are the result of transformations taking place in the invisible realm helps the lovers endure the challenges their egos can muster by insisting that the changes be visible and immediate.

The strength to see these changes through to completion is obtained from understanding the larger view of how they take place. Certainly, we are not always able, due to pressures of the ego, to see this larger view. Or, having seen it, we somehow slip back into seeing things from within the narrow dualities presented by the ego. We are accustomed to think in feudalistic terms, that the use of power is what makes things work in the world. The long view shows us, however, that the world, as fashioned by the ego, may indeed attain great power and stature, for a while. But nature itself works against those who use power, bravado, force, trickery, and arrogance. The *I Ching* uses the metaphor of a "meteoric rise leading to a meteoric fall" to describe the activities of the ego. When we have this clear view, we are able to cling, during moments when doubts threaten, to remembering that the Cosmos operates according to laws of harmony, and holds everything together by attraction. When we follow its ways, we find the correct solutions. This, together with only a little reflection, will return to our memory those events that have shown us that the Cosmos is beneficent, loving, and ever ready to come to our help. Often the only thing lacking is that we have forgotten to ask for help.

Chapter 12

The Pain and Perfection of Love

Learning to love in an entirely new way seems difficult, considering the many ingrained habits of mind that constitute the ego. The ego certainly has a vested interest in keeping them in place. It can be shrunk only by discipline and perseverance. A certain amount of pain accompanies this process, since it requires detaching oneself from those ego aspects which one has seen as making one successful in life.

Nevertheless, this task appears at that point in our lives when we are ready. As it is put in Hex. 47, Line 2, we become tired of the commonplaces of life, and seek to be of use in a Cosmic way. Of the three main paths that can lead to the development of the true self—money, health, and love—, love is probably the most difficult. However, we are never asked to take steps of development that we are not ready to take, or to trust what we have not been prepared for, through experience, to see is trustworthy.

We can prepare for the challenges of self-doubt, that will be initiated by the ego, by remembering that the path leads to the completion of the love relationship, when it flowers into understanding and humility. The lover needs to hold to this vision. Nothing can be achieved if we listen to the broken record played by the ego, "I can't make it, it's too difficult."

The challenges of bringing the relationship to completion involve the ego in yet another way. It constantly urges a mental approach in regard to the problems of relating. But such an approach only creates obstructions that remind us of our limitations as human beings. In regard to bringing the love relationship into being, we are constantly shown these limitations. In every area in which we attempt to apply power or force, we are rebuffed. In attempts to apply cunning or effort, we are made to fail. The Cosmic teacher is in charge, and leaves no aspect of our ego unnoticed. When we give way, relinquishing our cunning, effort, contriving, and the brilliance of our intellects, the Cosmos reaches its unseen hand out to open the channel between our inner self and our beloved. This invisible help is the unseen "vehicle for crossing" mentioned in Wilhelm's commentary to Hex. 64, Line 2. When we have done all we are meant to do, in the way of advancing and withdrawing, as mentioned earlier, we are meant to let go and leave the matter up to the Cosmos as to whether it is to happen or not. It is then that it can happen.

We need to remember, at times of suffering, that the one principle that governs the way the Cosmos works is love. This contrasts with the way the ego works through power: by trying to make things happen, by thinking harsh and angry thoughts, by making negative mental decisions that the partner *is* this or that way, by giving up and walking away, by holding onto perpetual anger and vindictiveness. Even when we try to fight the ego, in ourselves or in the other, it is the ego in us doing it, therefore it does not work. All uses of power empower the ego both in ourselves and the other. It is even an ego-use of power to *try* to love in order to heal rifts. The only way to make progress is to work at ridding oneself of one's ego and to say an inner No to the other's ego. The inner No must be said with firmness, but without any negative emotions attached. Then transformation occurs. Transformation is different from changes brought about through effort. Changes made through effort do not endure, whereas transformations occur on the atomic plane, and therefore endure.

The extent of our suffering is determined by how much pressure it takes to make us relinquish our ego, and to reduce our obstinacy to humility. This pressure is applied by fate as many times as necessary until we acknowledge that there is a greater reality beyond the titanic thought that we are in charge. All is put to rights when our humility begins to stay.

What more is required? In learning to love, we begin to see the part our consciousness plays in the equation of everything that happens. We see that doubts of our beloved rebound in his doubts of us, and that stored-up lists of transgressions rebound in his distrust of us. We see that all efforts to discipline the other create resistances which isolate us further from him. Through suffering at our own hands, we learn to say the inner No that brings help from the Cosmos.

Finding ourselves to be the author of our problems, we experience an enormous breakthrough, for then we also see that trust creates trust. The ego, with its demands and self-righteousness, its hopelessness, its tiring at persevering in our holding to the other's true self, its attempts to circumvent the gradual, step-by-step way by which all things worthwhile are organically achieved, is always cutting off our noses to spite our faces. Through repetition of these lessons, we finally see that true self-interest lies in freeing ourselves from measuring and testing, and from the need for vindication. We see that our pretense of achieving things through changes only leads to endless suffering, because it creates fates.

Suffering, we need to understand, is not part of the Cosmic harmony. It is the result of separating from our unity with the Cosmos by entertaining false ideas about the way things work, as for example, when we think that the Cosmos works in mechanical ways. We need to realize that it is the ego that thinks in mechanical terms and works in mechanical ways, and it automatically projects its way of thinking on the Cosmos. Once we realize that the Cosmos is a consciousness that is loving and caring, we also understand that fate and the suffering that accompanies it are neither punishments nor part of the way things are. They are the result of a false consciousness we have created through adopting false ideas. Their purpose is to awaken us to that fact, so that we can rid ourselves of the false mental programs. To rid ourselves of them, we always need the invisible help of the Cosmos. When we humbly recognize our need for help, help comes in whichever form it is needed in the situation.

When a partner who has taken on the role of the dependent one recognizes that the true source of all love is the Cosmos, and that he can also enjoy this love independently of the love partner, he becomes free of needing his partner in a dependent way. Self-development ultimately means placing one's dependence for all one's needs entirely on the Cosmos. Doing so reunites him with the Cosmic unity and harmony. No sooner does he do this than he starts to experience its help and nourishing presence. Immediately it removes the inner pressure he has been putting on his love partner, liberating him to respond to all the love coming through the inner channel. This ends his necessity to resist to the other's desire to constantly prove his love. It also ends his need to confront the dependent one with the fact that he is not the one meant to supply his needs. What the dominant one has been trying to say, all along through his resistance is, "I need you to be sufficient in yourself." It is dependence on the Cosmos that enables a person to be independent.

When the dependent one has finally shifted his dependency from the beloved to the Cosmos, the dominant one is suddenly freed to come forward. The necessary transformation now takes place. His eyes are gradually opened to see that any further resistance on his part is unnecessary. He is then drawn of his own accord by the attraction that is unleashed when the gift of love can be given freely, without pressure. The Cosmos opens all the remaining doors with ease and the lovers finally find their way to each other. This is the completion and perfection of love.

Chapter 13

Completion

The purpose of this book has been to investigate the love relationship with the view of following a path that will make it successful and enduring. By completing this path through the work of self-development, what is stated in Hex.13, Line 5 takes on meaning: "Men bound in fellowship first weep and lament, but afterward they laugh. After great struggles they succeed in meeting."

It does happen, however, that a particular love relationship, though it was meant to be, and though one partner will have persevered through all the challenges, will still fail to succeed. The time goes by when the great gift that has been offered the dominant one is taken away by the Cosmos. Opportunities, throughout our lives, are what the Cosmos offers, but in the end it is always up to us to exercise them. They do not remain available forever.

Despite the possibility of the failure of this particular relationship, the wooer must not look at it as his personal failure. He must be on guard against efforts of his ego to make him feel hopeless, and to bombard him with blame, "I knew it wouldn't work," "I should have done....(this)," or "I should have done....(that)." The ego will look at all one's good work as a failure, because its focus is only on the relationship, and not on the self-development one has achieved while working on the love relationship.

No good work is done for nothing. In the larger scheme of things, through doing his best, and through being consistently true to himself, the wooer finds himself suddenly freed from his assignment. For having endured the tests and challenges, he finds himself "kicked upstairs," as the expression goes, the way that some people, after enduring great adversity in the work place, find a much better job. The persevering person then finds that he is given a relationship that is even more suited to him, in all ways. This happens because the Cosmos is fair, and uses good to create good.

A person becomes freed when his work in a relationship is finished, meaning, he can let the other go without closing his heart, with full goodwill and wishes for the other's happiness. The relationship ends without his doing anything to end it.

Whether in the end their relationship completes itself in unity or separation, completion comes when the time is right, that is, when the Cosmos sees fit.

When the relationship is allowed to come to its natural end, the event is not looked at as a loss, especially for the one who has persevered. Instead of sadness or bitterness for all he has "invested" in the other, as the ego would put it, this person feels satisfied because an entire cornucopia of good things has poured out of his perseverance.

In this sort of completion, he is able to let the other go gently, with love. Then, instead of shrinking from life into an attitude of suspicion toward the Cosmos and its caring nature, such a person is able to care even more. Instead of spreading the bad news that loving another is something to be avoided at all costs, this person knows all the good that is implicit in loving. Instead of constantly reopening his wounds and reviewing his disappointments, so that he remains bruised, angry, and finger-pointing, he is healed completely from within, and can go on with his life in a healthy, loving way. The Cosmos loves such a person who can so retain his humility. It showers blessings on him in abundance.

What the outcome should be, in the long run, is not the important thing. What is important is that one sees the relationship through to its completion. The entire Hex. 53 shows the progression through time of a development that leads to completion of the true self. This progression is given in the image of a wild goose as it progresses from being an inexperienced gosling to a mature and fully developed goose: "The wild goose gradually draws near the cloud heights. Its feathers can be used for the sacred dance. Good fortune."

Wilhelm's commentary to this line reads, "Here life comes to its end. A man's work stands completed. The path rises high toward heaven, like the flight of wild geese when they have left the earth far behind. There they fly, keeping to the order of their flight in strict formation."

The metaphor here must not be taken too literally, because the goal of self-development is not the end of life, but the full recognition of one's total dependence on the Cosmos. It is this dependence which brings a person into harmony with the Cosmic consciousness. The image also shows that by bringing himself into this harmony, he is never alone. He finds people of like mind who have also worked on their self-development. Together, they continue with their lives.

Those who have learned to love and to trust in the Cosmos are rewarded, nourished, and aided, as needed, by wonderful experiences. Just as this chapter on completion was being written, such an event occurred in the life of a woman and her horse.

The relationship between this woman and her horse, which she brought up from a colt, was now 18 years old (the equivalent of about 72 human years). Her understanding of the horse's nature and her work with him had brought out the best in him. Throughout the eighteen years it was not always easy to give the horse everything he needed, but she held the view that once she had taken on the horse, she had taken on a commitment to see him through his life.

At this point, her horse was found to have a bone chip in its knee. She did everything possible to get it to heal, but just when this problem began to ease, the horse developed a serious intestinal obstruction. The new crisis continued for two days and nights during which she constantly walked the horse, as advised by the veterinarian. When the horse began to get better and the woman was resting, the horse somehow laid down and got stranded under a fence! Unfortunately, the intestinal obstruction had only moved further down in the intestine. In the meantime, walking the horse had re-inflamed its knee. The veterinarian said that there was no more to be done but to operate on the intestine, or else put the horse out of its misery. After some deliberation, the woman decided that it would be best to put the horse down, in view of the dangers of the operation, and the unsolvable knee problem. No decision could have been more difficult for this particular woman.

The next morning was one of those exquisite New England fall days, clear and warm, with radiant colors everywhere. The horse stood near a building in the sun, surrounded by a group of the woman's friends who were making every effort to comfort it. When the veterinarian arrived, the group accompanied the horse slowly to the spot, some distance away, where it would be buried. As they walked along, their attention was drawn to two enormous flocks of wild geese flying in V-shapes high in the sky. Curiously, their direction was not south, but exactly in the westward direction in which the group was walking. Hearing them honking so high overhead, intensified the hush that had developed. Just when they arrived at the intended burial place, the geese turned to the south and passed from sight. And so this gentle and good horse died, accompanied by this wonderful parallel event. Although none of these people knew of the above quoted passage from the *I Ching*, all of them felt that the geese flying by at that precise moment was a message from something that showed that what had happened was part of a greater and beautiful order.

Here the completion freed the woman from a relationship that had fulfilled its purpose, both for the horse and for the woman. And so, that is what completion is, and must be for those who follow the inner directive of love. This inner directive is to follow the path of one's destiny. It is the gift of love from the Cosmos that makes the journey possible, because it attracts the partner who is one's perfect complement. With the help of that love given to two people by the Cosmos, they recognize each others' true selves, even when they are kept as slaves under the tyranny of their egos.

In addition to love being our chief source of nourishment, love is a liberating energy. It is not given to put either partner in fetters. Love is also a healing energy for both partners. When it is allowed to flow freely, it spills over as a nourishing, liberating, and healing energy to everyone around.

That the Cosmos can show completion in the death of a horse, while the woman was freed to follow the path of her own unique destiny, is something wonderful to think about. Seeing such a completion as part of the harmonious workings of the Cosmos makes one think that maybe what we commonly call death and think of as the end of life, is really a transformation and release into an invisible form.

Other Books by Carol K. Anthony

A Guide to the I Ching

Third Edition, Revised

ISBN 0-9603832-4-7, Paperback, 336 pp.

This 1988 enlargement of Ms. Anthony's 1980 edition is now a classic interpretive manual to the *I Ching*, with a worldwide readership. It is available in English, Spanish, German, Portuguese, and Croatian.

This book was originally meant to accompany and explain the classic Wilhelm/Baynes translation of the *I Ching*, but as soon as it was published, it began to be used as an oracle in itself. Ms. Anthony has more than put the *I Ching* into modern language, she has dusted off its mirror surface, enabling it to reflect a person's inner truth, thereby aiding his true self to grow and flourish.

The Other Way Meditation Experiences Based on the I Ching

ISBN 0-9603832-5-5, Paperback, 264 pp.

Published in 1990, this book remains consistently popular since it provides many of the background meditations that led to Ms. Anthony's writing *A Guide to the I Ching*. The 250 meditations given here were the source of the many insights she received that clarified the *I Ching*'s obscure text. The book also describes the unusual meditation technique Ms. Anthony learned through working with the *I Ching*, and how it is a vehicle through which the Sage (the voice that speaks through the *I Ching*) can communicate.

The Philosophy of the I Ching,

Second Edition

ISBN 0-9603832-2-0, Paperback, 224 pp.

This new edition (1998) of a long-standing book first published in 1980, contains many new insights and reflections on the *I Ching*. In addition, it presents an entirely new way of consulting the oracle that allows the person to clarify the messages given. This book is particularly valuable for the first time *I Ching* user, as it gives him an overview of how the *I Ching* developed, and how its development was influenced by various schools of thought in China. It also explains its most common terms, such as the "Sage," the "Tao," the "superior man" and the "inferior man." It also explains its most common metaphors, such as "crossing the great water," "biting through," and a "big wagon for loading." Furthermore, it clarifies certain Cosmic principles, such as limitation, disengagement, and inner truth, and what the *I Ching* means by self-development.

I Ching—2002 The Oracle of the Cosmic Way

By Carol K. Anthony and Hanna Moog

ISBN 1-890764-0-0, Hardcover, 540 pp.

This new version of the ancient Chinese classic was revised under the guidance of the Sage that speaks through the oracle. It is an outgrowth of having asked one fundamental question: Since the *I Ching* is an oracle that can speak, why not ask the Sage that speaks through it to give us a new understanding of the hexagrams and lines? Crucial for the direct communication with the Sage was a method discovered by Ms. Anthony that allowed her to ask questions to which the

Sage could answer with either a full YES or NO, or a relative YES or NO. This method is available to everyone who wants to work directly with the Sage from a sincere wish to learn about the Cosmic Way.

The result of Ms. Anthony's and Ms. Moog's work with this new method, in addition to learning through meditations and dreams, has been the discovery of two distinctly different layers of text that make up the classic versions of the *I Ching*: (1) a superimposed and human-centered layer of text that reflects the values and aspirations of the feudal regimes of ancient China, and (2) a more hidden text that reflects the Cosmic principles that underly all life, and so, represent the Cosmic Way. This hidden text shows that the Cosmos has a beautiful order and works as a harmonious whole due to certain enduring principles: the equality and uniqueness of every aspect of the Cosmic whole, and a third quality: modesty, which results from knowing one's correct place in the Cosmic whole. These basic principles and a number of others make it possible for the Cosmos to work with a single force: love.

Recognizing these essential principles enables us to see with clarity what causes disharmony and chaos in the world. These causes are to be found in false ideas man has developed about the Cosmic Way and man's place in the whole. All of these false ideas constitute the layer of text that has been superimposed upon the original meanings of the hexagrams. They comprise the "feudal mindset"" of ancient China that imagined man to be the center of the universe. Obviously, this man-centered view of the universe still exists today in all the feudally derived cultures of the world.

Bringing oneself into harmony with the Cosmos means returning to modesty. Doing so restores a person to his original wholeness. How is this to be achieved? First, through recognizing the false ideas and values we have accepted from this ancient mindset. Second, through firmly rejecting each of these ideas, which have become installed in our psyches as a false mental program. The *I Ching—2002* shows, step by step, how this *inner* work is to be carried out. It also enables a person to clearly distinguish his true self from the impostor "self'" created by the man-centered view. Reuniting with the Cosmos equals reuniting with our true self. Doing the inner work not only brings us into harmony with ourselves and those around us, it also removes the causes of illnesses, both of the mind and body.

Seeing the effects of these false ideas makes us realize that illnesses are neither to be endured nor to be fought, but that they are reactions of our own natures to thoughts that slander our natural wholeness. When we deprogram them, the illness heals.

The *I Ching—2002* makes us aware of the responsibility we hold for the way we use language. Words that falsely describe the true nature of things have a far more destructive effect than we commonly think. The *I Ching* oracle, we are made to realize, has been given to humans to teach them the Cosmic Way, not the human way created by the man-centered view.